Learn to crochet

GRANNY SQUARES & FLOWER MOTIFS

25 PROJECTS TO GET YOU STARTED

Nicki Trench

CICO BOOKS

LONDON NEW YORK

Published in 2018 by CICO Books
an imprint of Ryland Peters & Small Ltd
20–21 Jockey's Fields, London WC1R 4BW

www.rylandpeters.com

10 9 8 7 6 5 4 3 2 1

Patterns in this book have previously been published in the titles *Crochet Basics*, *Crocheted Scarves and Cowls*, *Cute and Easy Crochet*, *Cute and Easy Crochet with Flowers*, *Cute and Easy Crocheted Baby Clothes*, *Cute and Easy Crocheted Cosies*, or *Geek Chic Crochet*.

A CIP catalogue record for this book is available from the British Library.

ISBN: 978 1 78249 567 3

Printed in China

Editor: Marie Clayton
Pattern checker: Jane Czaja
Designer: Alison Fenton
Photographers: Caroline Arber, Terry Benson, James Gardiner, Gavin Kingcome, Martin Norris, Penny Wincer
Stylists: Alison Davidson, Nel Haynes, Sophie Martell, Rob Merrett, Luis Peral-Aranda, Jo Thornhill

Art director: Sally Powell
Production controller: Mai-Ling Collyer
Publishing manager: Penny Craig
Publisher: Cindy Richards

Learn to crochet
GRANNY SQUARES & FLOWER MOTIFS

Contents

Introduction 6
Equipment 8
Techniques 10

Chapter 1
FOR THE HOME 28

Bunting 30
Wash cloth 32
Camellia blanket 34
Crown-edged cushion cover 37
Sweetheart blanket 40
Baby cloths 42
Hexagon flower throw 44
Buggy blanket 47
Oven cloths 50
Vintage-style vase coaster 52
Hexagon blanket 54
Intarsia heart cushion 57
Triangle blanket 60

Chapter 2
TO WEAR 64

Child's granny square sweater 66
Crop top 70
Circles cardigan 72
Daisy scarf 74
Stars scarf 76
Jewel cowl 78
Triangles scarf 80
Chunky squares scarf 82

Chapter 3
TO CARRY AND COVER 84

Patchwork bag 86
Sunglasses case 88
Multicoloured laptop cover 90
Patchwork sewing machine
   cover 92

Suppliers 94
Index 95
Acknowledgements 96

Introduction

Learning to crochet may be one of the most satisfying skills you ever learn. It's creative, very fulfilling, relaxing and been proven to lower your blood pressure too! Making granny squares and motifs is uniquely special to crochet and a really great way to learn stitches and shaping. It also means that you can go wild with your colour choices.

In this collection we have chosen a wide variety of projects to inspire you to crochet. There are projects for a variety of skill levels from beginner to more intermediate, so once you've achieved some of the simpler projects, there are others to choose from that will take you to the next level.

When first starting out, I always recommend you choose a project that you love. That way you'll be motivated to drive yourself forward and finish – never give up! In this book you'll find a comprehensive Techniques section to guide you through the techniques and stitches, and we also have a list of all the equipment you need, as well as a Suppliers list which includes places where you will be able to buy all the yarns and hooks you need to start.

For the complete beginner, try something for your home – the Crown-edged Cushion Cover has a lovely and easy pattern to follow, or something in a very similar pattern is the Traditional Square in the Baby Cloths project. One of my favourite projects to wear is the Chunky Squares Scarf – this crochets really quickly and is a very easy project to make.

Once you have moved off the beginner's stage, there are some great projects to move on to. Try the Multicoloured Laptop Cover, the beautiful Hexagon Flower Throw, and the Child's Granny Square Sweater. For those more advanced, there is the gorgeous Sweetheart Blanket, the colourful and bright Buggy Blanket or the beautiful silk Triangle Blanket.

Whether you are just starting out in your journey into the world of crochet or you are a more seasoned crocheter I hope you enjoy the inspirational and interesting projects in this book. There is something here for everyone.

Equipment

You don't need a lot of equipment to make the projects in this book, but if you are new to crochet, the information here will help you make sure you've got everything you need before you begin.

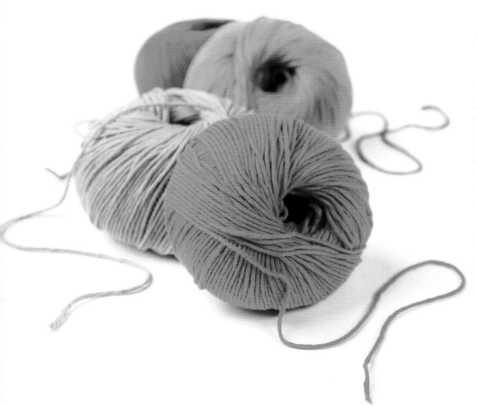

YARN

The yarn type and shades used are listed for each pattern. For projects which only require small amounts of yarn you may choose to use some from your yarn stash instead. If you want to use a different yarn from the one in the pattern, use the information given about the yarn (weight, material, length per ball, weight of ball) to find a suitable substitute, or ask at your local yarn store.

CROCHET HOOKS

Crochet hooks come in a variety of sizes and you'll be guided by the pattern and the thickness of yarn as to which size you need. If you find that your stitches are too loose or too tight, try experimenting with a slightly smaller or larger hook. If you are purchasing your first hook for practise, then use a double-knitting weight yarn and a 4mm (US size G/6) crochet hook. Whichever type of hook you choose, it's important that it has a good smooth tip, and it's worth trying out different brands to see which you like best before making a purchase. I keep my hooks in a hook holder so I don't lose them, or in an old-fashioned wooden pencil stand where they are easily accessible.

OTHER EQUIPMENT

STITCH MARKERS

These are used to mark the first stitch of every round. You can buy different types, but I find that a length of contrasting crochet cotton or thin yarn also works really well – it is easy to weave it in and out of each round and it doesn't get in your way – or try using a safety pin. At the end of a completed round, loop the stitch marker through the loop on the hook thus marking your first stitch of the next round. Counting your stitches after each round helps to make sure you are completing the correct number.

YARN SEWING NEEDLES

These come in various sizes, but all have large eyes for easy threading of yarn, and a blunt end which will not split the stitches when you are sewing up your work.

SHARP SCISSORS

You will need these for cutting yarn after finishing a piece and when sewing up. It is tempting to break yarn with your hands, but this can pull the stitches out of shape.

TAPE MEASURE

A tape measure is an inexpensive and essential tool for a crocheter. You will need it to measure your crochet pieces and your tension squares.

PINS

I always pin my crochet pieces together before I sew them up or make a crochet seam. Rustproof, glass-headed or T-headed quilter's pins can be used to pin crocheted pieces together. Bright-coloured tops make it easy to spot the pins against the crocheted fabric, so you don't leave any behind!

Techniques

In this section there are instructions for all the basic crochet techniques you will need to make the projects. If you can't find the recommended yarn, you can substitute a different yarn of the same type – so another Aran (worsted) to replace an Aran (worsted), or a DK (light worsted) to replace a DK (light worsted) – but you will need to check the tension carefully.

Holding the hook

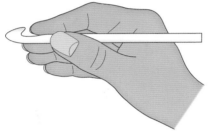

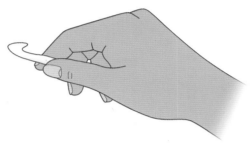

Pen position Pick up your hook as though you are picking up a pen or pencil. Keeping the hook held loosely between your fingers and thumb, turn your hand so that the palm is facing up and the hook is balanced in your hand and resting in the space between your index finger and your thumb.

Knife position If I'm using a very large hook and chunky yarn, then I may sometimes change and use the knife position. I crochet a lot and I've learned that it's important to take care not to damage your arm or shoulder by being too tense. Make sure you're always relaxed when crocheting and take breaks.

Holding the yarn

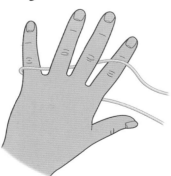

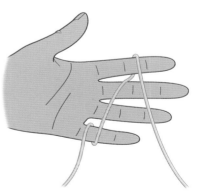

1 Pick up the yarn with your little finger in the opposite hand to your hook, with your palm facing upwards and with the short end in front. Turn your hand to face downwards, with the yarn on top of your index finger and under the other two fingers and wrapped right around the little finger, as shown above.

2 Turn your hand to face you, ready to hold the work in your middle finger and thumb. Keeping your index finger only at a slight curve, hold the work or the slip knot using the same hand, between your middle finger and your thumb and just below the crochet hook and loop/s on the hook.

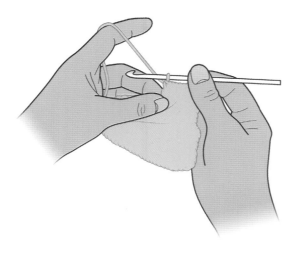

Holding your hook, yarn and crochet

Keep your index finger, with the yarn draped over it, at a slight curve, and hold your work (or the slip knot) using the same hand, between your middle finger and your thumb and just below the crochet hook and the loop/s on the hook.

As you draw the loop through the hook, release the yarn on the index finger to allow the loop to stay loose on the hook. If you tense your index finger, the yarn will become too tight and pull the loop on the hook too tight for you to draw the yarn through.

Some left-handers learn to crochet like right-handers, but others learn with everything reversed – with the hook in the left hand and the yarn in the right.

Yarn round hook (yrh)

To create a stitch, catch the yarn from behind with the hook pointing upwards. As you gently pull the yarn through the loop on the hook, turn the hook so it faces downwards and slide the yarn through the loop. The loop on the hook should be kept loose enough for the hook to slide through easily.

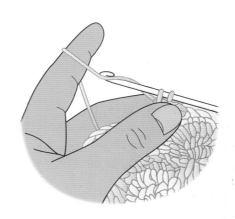

Making a slip knot

The simplest way is to make a circle with the yarn, so that the loop is facing downwards.

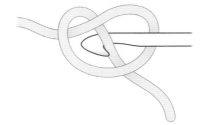

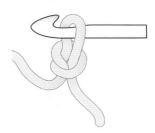

1 Make a circle in the yarn, as shown above.

2 In one hand hold the circle at the top where the yarn crosses, and let the tail drop down at the back so that it falls across the centre of the loop. With your free hand or the tip of a crochet hook, pull a loop through the circle.

3 Put the hook into the loop and pull gently so that it forms a loose loop on the hook.

Chain (ch)

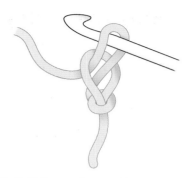

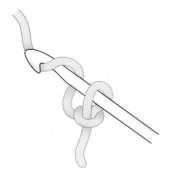

1 Make a slip knot and put it on the hook. Using the hook, wrap the yarn round the hook ready to pull it through the loop on the hook.

2 Pull through, creating a new loop on the hook. Continue in this way to create a chain of the required length.

Chain ring

If you are crocheting a round shape, one way of starting off is by crocheting a number of chains following the instructions in your pattern, and then joining them into rings, or a circle.

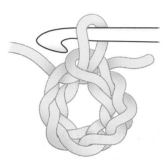

1 To join the chain into a circle, insert the crochet hook into the first chain that you made (not into the slip knot), yarn round hook.

2 Pull the yarn through the chain and through the loop on your hook at the same time, thereby creating a slip stitch and forming a circle. You now have a chain ring ready to work stitches into as instructed in the pattern.

Chain space (ch sp)

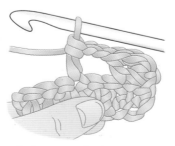

1 A chain space is the space that has been made under a chain in the previous round or row, and falls in between other stitches.

2 Stitches into a chain space are made directly into the hole/space created under the chain and not into the chain stitches themselves.

Working into a ring

  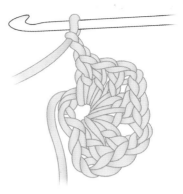

1 After making the chain ring you'll be instructed to make a number of chains to bring your work up to the right height for the first stitch of the first round.

2 Keep an eye on where the centre of the ring is. I usually stick my finger into the hole to define it – this can be neatened up later when sewing in ends.

3 As you are making the stitches and chains to create this first round you may feel that you are running out of space in the ring. If so, ease the stitches round so they are more bunched up, which will give you more space in the ring, and take care not to make your new stitches over the top of the first stitches or chains made in this round.

Working into top of stitch

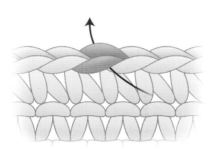

Unless otherwise directed, insert the hook under both of the 2 loops on top of the stitch – this is the standard technique.

Slip stitch (ss)

A slip stitch doesn't create any height and is often used as the last stitch to create a smooth and even round or row.

1 To make a slip stitch: first put the hook through the work, yarn round hook.

2 Pull the yarn through both the work and through the loop on the hook at the same time, so you will have 1 loop on the hook.

Making rounds

When working in rounds the work is not turned, so you are always working from one side. Depending on the pattern you are working, a 'round' can be made into a square. Some rounds are started by making one or more chains to create the height you need for the stitch you are working:

Double crochet = 1 chain
Half treble crochet = 2 chains
Treble crochet = 3 chains

Work the required stitches to complete the round. At the end of the round, slip stitch into the top of the chain to close the round.

Making rows

When making straight rows you turn the work at the end of each row and make a turning chain to create the height you need for the stitch you are working with, as for making rounds.

Double crochet = 1 chain
Half treble crochet = 2 chains
Treble crochet = 3 chains

Using a stitch marker

When working crochet in rounds, you join each round with a slip stitch (see page 15). After completing the base ring, place a stitch marker to denote the beginning of the round. When you've made a round and reached the point where the stitch marker is, work this stitch, take out the stitch marker from the previous round and put it back into the first stitch/chain of the new round. A safety pin makes a good stitch marker.

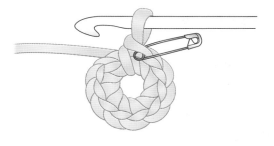

Working in the round

Once you have created a ring and worked into the ring (see page 13), you will need to continue working in rounds. This illustration shows working in the round in treble (tr).

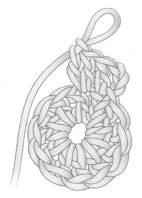

1 Work 3ch (this counts as 1tr). Work 1tr in the same place as the last slip stitch.

2 The next stitch is the one directly next to the stitch into which you've just made a treble. Make sure you pick up both loops of this stitch. This example shows 2tr made into the same stitch – making two trebles into the same stitch creates an increase.

Joining rounds with a slip stitch

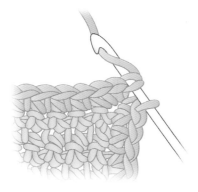

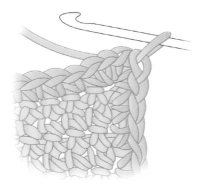

1 After completing the last stitch of the round – here worked in double crochet – insert the hook into the top of the first stitch, then yarn round hook.

2 Pull the yarn through both the stitch and loop on the hook to join the 2 stitches (1 loop on hook). Fasten off the yarn (see page 24).

Creating a square

A square is created by making stitches and chain spaces into the same space or stitches, which makes a fan shape and creates the corner. This is the basis of all corners on crochet square motifs, although some use different stitches and patterns.

1 Slip stitch across the next two stitches as instructed in the pattern – the slip stitches don't create any height, they just take the yarn across the stitches towards the chain space, where the pattern for the next round will start.

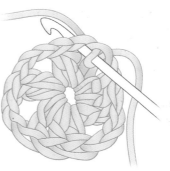

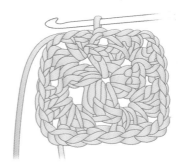

2 To make the slip stitches, insert the hook into each of the next two stitches, picking up both loops of each stitch (see page 13). Now, slip stitch into the chain space.

3 To make a corner from a circle, you need to make a group of stitches into the same chain space.

4 If you continue with the pattern you will create four corners and so will have made a square from a circle.

Joining new yarn at the end of a row or round

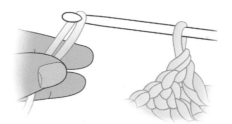

1 Do not fasten off, but keep the loop of the old yarn on the hook. Drop the tail and catch a loop of the strand of the new yarn with the crochet hook.

2 Pull the new yarn through the loop on the hook, keeping the old loop drawn tight.

Joining in new yarn after fastening off

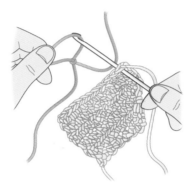

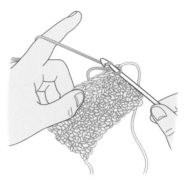

1 Fasten off the old colour (see page 24). Make a slip knot with the new colour (see page 11). Insert the hook into the stitch at the beginning of the next row, then through the slip knot.

2 Pull the loop of the slip knot through to the front of the work. Carry on working using the new colour, following the instructions in the pattern.

Enclosing a yarn tail

You may find that the yarn tail gets in the way as you work; you can enclose this into the stitches as you go by placing the tail at the back as you wrap the yarn. This also saves having to sew this tail end in later.

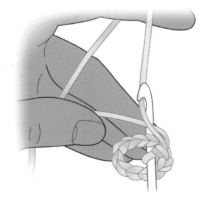

How to measure a tension (gauge) square

Using the hook and the yarn recommended in the pattern, make a number of chains to measure approximately 15cm (6in). Working in the stitch pattern given for the tension measurements, work enough rows to form a square. Fasten off.

Take a ruler, place it horizontally across the square, and using pins, mark a 10cm (4in) area. Repeat vertically to form a 10cm (4in) square on the fabric. Count the number of stitches and rows and compare against the given tension. If your numbers match the pattern, use this size of hook. If you have more stitches, try a larger hook. If you have fewer stitches, try a smaller hook. Make squares using different sized hooks until you have matched the tension in the pattern.

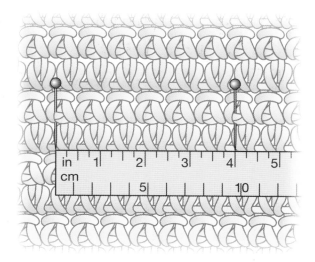

Double crochet (dc)

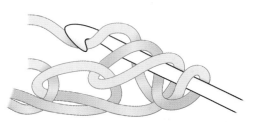

1 Insert the hook into your work, yarn round hook and pull the yarn through the work only. You will then have 2 loops on the hook.

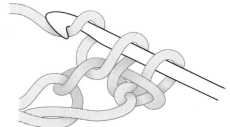

2 Yarn round hook again and pull through the 2 loops on the hook. You will then have 1 loop left on the hook.

Half treble crochet (htr)

1 Before inserting the hook into the work, wrap the yarn round the hook and put the hook through the work with the yarn wrapped around.

2 Yarn round hook again and pull through the first loop on the hook. You now have 3 loops on the hook.

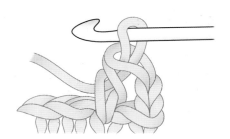

3 Yarn round hook and pull the yarn through all 3 loops. You will be left with 1 loop on the hook.

Treble (tr)

1 Before inserting the hook into the work, wrap the yarn round the hook. Put the hook through the work with the yarn wrapped around, yarn round hook again and pull through the first loop on the hook. You now have 3 loops on the hook.

2 Yarn round hook again, pull the yarn through the first 2 loops on the hook. You now have 2 loops on the hook.

3 Pull the yarn through 2 loops again. You will be left with 1 loop on the hook. The height of each stitch is called a 'post'.

Double treble (dtr)

Yarn round hook twice, insert hook into the stitch, yarn round hook, pull a loop through (4 loops on the hook), yarn round hook, pull the yarn through 2 stitches (3 loops on the hook), yarn round hook, pull the yarn through the next 2 stitches (2 loops on the hook), yarn round hook, pull a loop through the last 2 loops. You will be left with 1 loop on the hook.

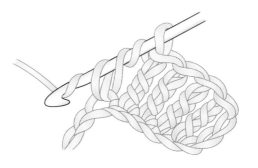

Double crochet

Half treble crochet

Treble crochet

Triple treble (trtr)

Triple trebles are 'tall' stitches and are an extension on the basic treble stitch. They need a turning chain of 5 chains.

1 Yarn round hook three times, insert the hook into the stitch or space. Yarn round hook, pull the yarn through the work (5 loops on the hook).

2 Yarn round hook, pull the yarn through the first 2 loops on the hook (4 loops on the hook).

3 Yarn round hook, pull the yarn through the first 2 loops on the hook (3 loops on the hook).

4 Yarn round hook, pull the yarn through the first 2 loops on the hook (2 loops on the hook). Yarn round hook, pull the yarn through the 2 loops on the hook. You will be left with 1 loop on the hook.

Front post crochet

Raised stitches are created by making stitches around the 'posts' of the stitches below (in the previous round/row) – the posts are also sometimes called 'stems' or 'stalks'. Here we are working around the front post, in double crochet (dc/rf).

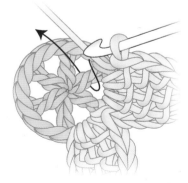

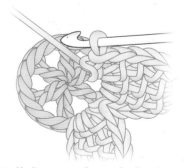

1 Insert the hook from the front and around the post (the stem) of next double from right to left.

2 Yarn round hook, pull the yarn through the work, yarn round hook.

3 Pull the yarn through the 2 loops on the hook. One front post double crochet completed, and 1 loop left on the hook.

Increasing

Make two or three stitches into one stitch or space from the previous row. The illustration shows a treble crochet increase being made.

Decreasing

You can decrease by either missing the next stitch and continuing to crochet, or by crocheting two or more stitches together. The basic technique for crocheting stitches together is the same, no matter which stitch you are using. The illustrations show a decrease worked in double crochet.

Double crochet two stitches together (dc2tog)

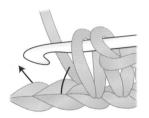

1 Insert the hook in the first stitch, yarn round hook and pull through (2 loops on the hook). Insert the hook in the next stitch.

2 Yarn round hook and pull through (3 loops on the hook). Yarn round hook again and pull through all 3 loops on the hook. You will be left with 1 loop on the hook.

Loop stitch

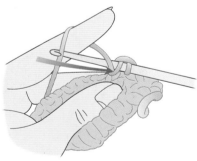

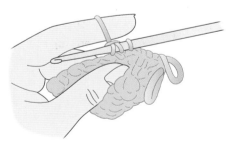

1 With the yarn over your left index finger, insert the hook into the next stitch and draw two strands through the stitch (take the first strand from under the index finger and at the same time take the second strand from over the index finger).

2 Pull the yarn to tighten the loop, forming a 2.5cm (1in) loop on the index finger. Remove your finger from the loop, put the loop to the back of the work, yarn round hook and pull through three loops on the hook (1 loop stitch made on the back of the work).

Picot

A picot is a little bobble texture that is often used to create little points along the outer edge of an edging. The illustrations show a three-chain picot.

1 Make 14ch.
Row 1: 1dc in second ch from hook, 1dc in each ch to end.
Row 2: 1ch, 1dc in each of next 2 sts, 3tr in next st, *1dc in each of the next 3 sts, 3tr in next st: rep from * twice more, 2dc in each of last 2 sts.
Row 3 (picot row): 1ch, 1dc in each of next 2 dc, 1dc in top of next tr, *3ch.

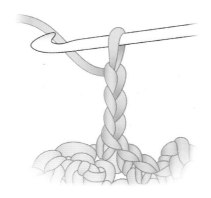

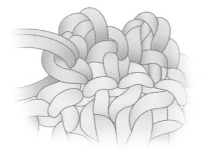

2 Ss in third ch from hook (one picot made). 1dc in top of next tr.

3 Rep from * once more, 3ch, ss in third ch from hook (picot made)**, 1dc in each of next 3 dc, 1dc in top of next tr; rep from * ending last rep at **, 1dc in each of last two dc.

Puff stitch

A puff stitch is a padded stitch worked by creating several loops on the hook before completing the stitch. Sometimes a chain is worked at the end to secure the puff stitch. A basic puff stitch is worked as follows: [Yarn round hook, insert the hook in the stitch or space specified in the pattern, yarn round hook and pull a loop through] the number of times stated in the pattern, keeping all the loops quite loose. Yarn round hook, and draw through all loops on the hook.

Clusters

Clusters are groups of stitches, with each stitch only partly worked and then all joined at the end to form one stitch that creates a particular pattern and shape. They are most effective when made using a longer stitch such as a treble.

Two-treble cluster (2trCL)

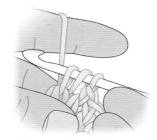

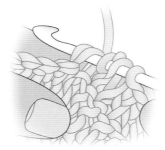

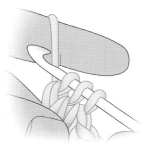

1 Yarn round hook, insert the hook in the stitch (or space). Yarn round hook, pull the yarn through the work (3 loops on the hook).

2 Yarn round hook, pull the yarn through 2 loops on the hook (2 loops on the hook). Yarn round hook, insert the hook in the same stitch (or space).

3 Yarn round hook, pull the yarn through the work (4 loops on the hook). Yarn round hook, pull the yarn through 2 loops on the hook (3 loops on the hook).

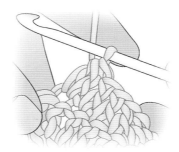

4 Yarn round hook, pull the yarn through all 3 loops on the hook (1 loop on hook). One two-treble cluster made.

Three-treble cluster (3trCL)

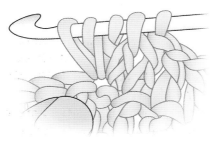

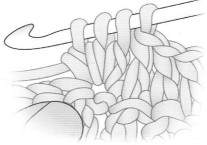

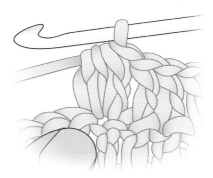

1 Work as 2trCL to end of step 3. Yarn round hook, insert the hook in the same stitch (or space), yarn round hook, pull the yarn through the work (5 loops on the hook).

2 Yarn round hook, pull the yarn through 2 loops on the hook (4 loops on the hook).

3 Yarn round hook, pull the yarn through all 4 loops on the hook (1 loop on the hook). One three-treble cluster made.

Intarsia

Before you start on the pattern for the Sweetheart Blanket (page 40) or the Intarsia Heart Cushion (page 57), print off the relevant chart and wind off two balls of the main colour (MC) from the larger ball. Cut a separate strand of yarn about 100cm (40in) long to be used for the indentation at the top of the heart.

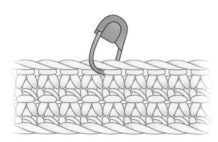

1 Using MC (ball 1), make the Foundation chain then work in double crochet for the one-colour rows leading up to the motif, making sure you make the chain at the beginning of each row for the height of the stitch. When you are ready to start the motif, place a stitch marker in the centre stitch of the row.

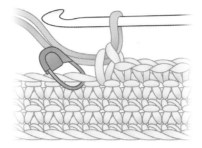

2 Work the beginning of the row in MC, to the stitch before the stitch marker.
Motif row 1 (RS): Join in the contrast colour (CC) in the stitch before the stitch marker.

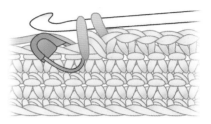

3 Drop MC (ball 1), insert the hook in the next stitch (with stitch marker), and pull the CC yarn through the stitch.

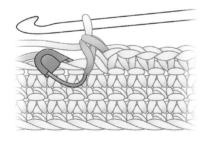

4 Take MC (ball 2), drop CC, then pull the MC yarn through both loops to complete the double crochet stitch.

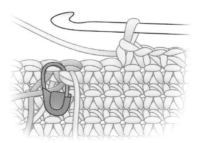

5 Continue in double crochet with MC (ball 2), to the end of the row, leaving MC (ball 1) and CC behind and sitting at the back of the work (on the wrong side).
Motif row 2 (WS): Make the chain in MC (ball 2), then double crochet up to two stitches before the CC stitch (with the stitch marker).

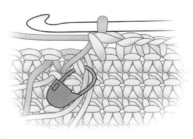

6 Insert the hook into the next stitch of MC (ball 2), and pull CC through the stitch. Drop MC (ball 2) and bring the strand of MC (ball 2) over the top of the work to drape on the wrong side (facing you). Bring up the strand of CC loosely across and join by pulling it through both loops on the hook.

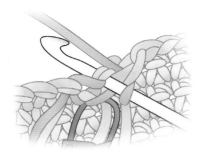
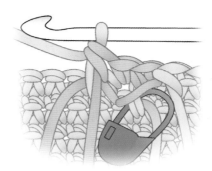

7 Insert the hook into the next stitch, gently pushing the strand of CC out of the way.

8 Complete the stitch using CC. Make one double crochet in the next stitch using CC. Insert the hook in the next CC stitch of the motif, and pull CC through the stitch. Drop CC, keeping the strand of yarn on the wrong side (facing you), pick up MC (ball 1) and complete the stitch in MC. All strands should be on the wrong side (facing you).

Fastening off

When you have finished crocheting, you need to fasten off the stitches to stop all your work unravelling.

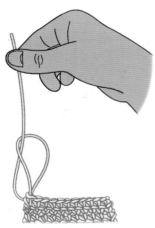

1 Pull up the final loop of the last stitch to make it bigger. Cut the yarn, leaving a tail of approx 10cm (4in). Pull the tail all the way through the loop and pull the loop up tightly.

Sewing in yarn ends

Weave ends in and out of the work over approx 5cm (2in) on the wrong side of the crochet, keeping to the same area of colour in the design.

Blocking

Crochet can tend to curl so to make flat pieces stay flat you may need to block them. Pin the piece out to the correct size and shape on the ironing board, then cover with a cloth and press or steam gently (depending on the type of yarn) and allow to dry completely.

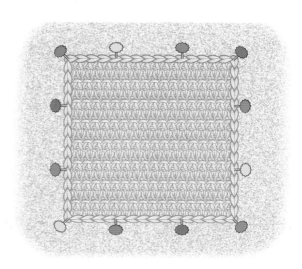

Making a double crochet seam

With a double crochet seam you join two pieces together using a crochet hook and working a double crochet stitch through both pieces, instead of sewing them together with a tail of yarn and a yarn sewing needle. This makes a quick and strong seam and gives a slightly raised finish to the edging. For a less raised seam, follow the same basic technique, but work each stitch in slip stitch rather than double crochet.

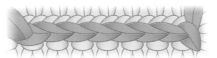

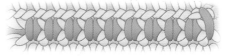

1 Start by lining up the two pieces with wrong sides together. Insert the hook in the top 2 loops of the stitch of the first piece, then into the corresponding stitch on the second piece.

2 Complete the double crochet stitch as normal and continue on the next stitches as directed in the pattern. This gives a raised effect if the double crochet stitches are made on the right side of the work.

3 You can work with the wrong side of the work facing (with the pieces right side facing) if you don't want this effect and it still creates a good strong join.

Backstitch

This is a simple sewing stitch that can be used to join squares together. Working from left to right, bring the needle up from the back of the fabric, one stitch length to the left of the start of the stitching line. Insert it to the right, at the end of the stitching line, then bring it up again one stitch length to the left of the point from which it first emerged. Pull the thread through. For the next stitch, insert the needle at the left-hand end of the previous stitch. Continue to end.

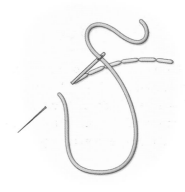

Making an oversewn seam

An oversewn join gives a nice flat seam and is the most simple and common joining technique.

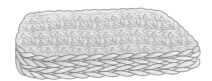
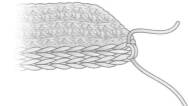

1 Thread a yarn sewing needle with the yarn you're using in the project. Place the pieces to be joined with right sides together.

2 Insert the needle in one corner in the top loops of the stitches of both pieces and pull up the yarn, leaving a tail of about 5cm (2in). Go into the same place with the needle and pull up the yarn again; repeat two or three times to secure the yarn at the start of the seam.

3 Join the pieces together by taking the needle through the loops at the top of corresponding stitches on each piece to the end. Fasten off the yarn at the end as in step 2.

Backing with fabric

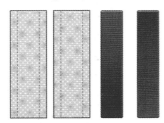
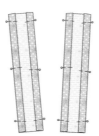

1 Measure the crochet and cut out the lining the same size plus an extra 1.5cm (⅝in) on each side for the hem.

2 Press a 1.5cm (⅝in) wide hem to the wrong side along each edge and pin in place.

3 Place the lining with the hem side down onto the wrong side of the crochet. Pin and then hand sew the lining to the crocheted piece using a simple whip stitch. Remove the pins.

Lining crochet with fabric

It's not always necessary to line a crochet bag or case, but in some projects a lining will prevent the contents poking through gaps in the stitch pattern. The general method is given here.

1 Cut two pieces of lining fabric to the same size as the crocheted piece, plus an extra 1.5cm (⅝in) allowance for seams on the sides and bottom and an extra 2.5cm (1in) at the top. Pin the fabric pieces right sides together and machine sew the side and bottom seams. Trim across the bottom corners and press out the seams.

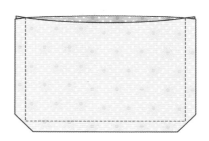

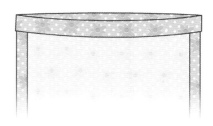

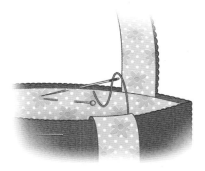

2 Turn the top edge of the lining over to the wrong side by 2.5cm (1in) and press.

3 Insert the lining into the item with wrong sides of crochet and lining together and pin in place around the top edge. Hand-sew the lining to the crochet around the top edge, stitching across any handles if they are being inserted between the lining and the bag.

Abbreviations

[ ]	square parentheses indicate a repeated stitch sequence	dc2tog	double crochet 2 stitches together	rep	repeat
				RS	right side of work
*	asterisk indicates beginning of a repeated section	dc3tog	double crochet 3 stitches together	sp(s)	space(s)
				ss	slip stitch
		dtr	double treble	st(s)	stitch(es)
alt	alternate	g	gram(s)	tog	together
approx	approximately	htr	half treble	tr	treble
beg	beginning	htr2tog	half treble 2 stitches together	tr3tog	treble 3 stitches together
CC	contrast colour				
ch	chain	in	inch(es)	trCL	treble cluster
ch sp(s)	chain space(s)	m	metre(s)	trtr	triple treble
cm	centimetre(s)	MC	main colour	WS	wrong side of work
cont	continu(e)(ing)	oz	ounce(s)	yd(s)	yard(s)
dc	double crochet	patt	pattern	yrh	yarn round hook
		rem	remaining		

Crochet stitch conversion chart

Crochet stitches are worked in the same way in the UK and the USA, but the stitch names are not the same and identical names are used for different stitches.

Here is a list of the UK terms used in this book, and the equivalent US terms.

UK TERM	US TERM
double crochet (dc)	single crochet (sc)
half treble (htr)	half double crochet (hdc)
treble (tr)	double crochet (dc)
double treble (dtr)	treble (tr)
triple treble (trtr)	double treble (dtr)
tension	gauge
yarn round hook (yrh)	yarn over hook (yoh)

CHAPTER 1

FOR THE *Home*

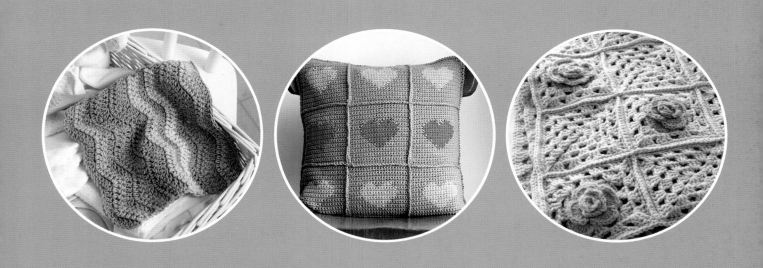

Bunting

Brighten up any room of the house with some traditional bunting! The flowers between the flags give it a wonderfully feminine feel.

YARN
Rooster Almerino DK, 50% baby alpaca, 50% merino wool DK (light worsted) yarn, approx 113m (124yd) per 50g (1¾oz) ball
1 ball each of:
211 Brighton Rock (pink) (A)
215 Lilac Sky (pale lilac) (B)
216 Pier (pale green) (C)
217 Beach (turquoise) (D)
218 Starfish (orange) (E)
219 Sandcastle (pale yellow) (F)

HOOK AND EQUIPMENT
4mm (US size G/6) crochet hook
Yarn sewing needle

TENSION
Each flag measures 18.5cm (7¼in) along each side, using a 4mm (US size G/6) hook.

MEASUREMENTS
The finished bunting measures approx 111cm (43½in) long, excluding the end ties.

ABBREVIATIONS
See page 27.

Flags
(make 6, using any 3 of the 6 colours – A, B, C, D, E, F – for each)
Using first colour, make 4ch, join with a ss in first ch to form a ring.
Round 1 (RS): 3ch (counts as 1tr), 3tr in ring, *[3ch, 4tr in ring] twice, 3ch, join with a ss in top of first 3-ch.
Fasten off first colour. Cont in rounds with RS always facing.
Round 2: Join second colour with a ss in any 3-ch sp, 3ch (counts as 1tr), [4tr, 1ch, 5tr] in same sp, *1ch, [5tr, 1ch, 5tr] in next 3-ch sp; rep from * once more, 1ch, join with a ss in top of first 3-ch.
Fasten off second colour.
Round 3: Join third colour with a ss in 1-ch sp between any two 5-tr corner groups, 3ch (counts as 1tr), [1tr, 2ch, 2tr] in same sp, *1tr in each of next 5 tr, miss 1-ch sp, 1tr in each of next 5 tr, [2tr, 2ch, 2tr] in next 1-ch sp (corner); rep from * once more, 1tr in each of next 5 tr, miss 1-ch sp, 1tr in each of next

5 tr, join with a ss in top of first 3-ch. Do not fasten off, but cont working with third colour to complete flag.

Round 4: 1ss in next tr, 1ss in next 2-ch sp (corner), 3ch (counts as 1tr), [2tr, 3ch, 3tr] in same sp, *miss 1 tr, [3tr in next tr, miss 2 tr] 4 times, 3tr in next tr, [3tr, 3ch, 3tr] in next 2-ch sp (corner); rep from * once more, miss 1 tr, [3tr in next tr, miss next 2 tr] 4 times, 3tr in next tr, join with a ss in top of first 3-ch.

Round 5: 1ss in each of next 2 tr, 1ss in next 3-ch sp (corner), 3ch (counts as 1tr), [2tr, 3ch, 3tr] in same sp, *3tr in each of next 6 sps between 3-tr groups, [3tr, 3ch, 3tr] in next 3-ch sp corner; rep from * once more, 3tr in each of next 6 sps between 3-tr groups, join with a ss in top of first 3-ch.

Round 6: 1ch, 1dc in same place as last ss, 1dc in each of next 2 tr, 3dc in next 3-ch sp (corner), [1dc in each of next 24 tr, 3dc in next 3-ch sp] twice, 1dc in each of next 21 tr, join with a ss in first dc, 1ss in each of next 2 dc.
Fasten off.

Top edge:
With RS of first flag facing and using A, join yarn with a ss in centre dc of any 3-dc corner group of first flag, 1ch, 1dc in same place as ss, *1dc in each dc up to next 3-dc corner group, 1dc in each of first 2 dc of group, take next flag and with RS facing, work 1dc in centre dc of any 3-dc corner group (this joins flags together); rep from * until all flags are attached. Do not fasten off, but cont to work first tie as follows.

First tie:
Cont with A, make approx 59ch or until tie measures 30.5cm (12in) from edge of last flag.
Fasten off.

Second tie:
With RS facing, join A with a ss in top of first dc at start of top edge, make approx 59ch or until chain measures 30.5cm (12in) to match first tie.
Fasten off.

Flowers
(make 7, using any 2 of the 6 colours – A, B, C, D, E, F – for each)
Using first colour, make 6ch, join with a ss in first dc to form a ring.
Round 1: 1ch, 15dc in ring, enclosing yarn tail inside each dc around ring. Break off first colour, but do not fasten off.

Round 2: Join in second colour with 1ss in first dc in Round 1, *3ch, 1tr in each of next 2 dc, 3ch, 1ss in next dc st; rep from * 4 more times, working last ss in first dc. (5 petals)
Fasten off.
Pull yarn tail to close up centre hole and sew in ends.

Making up and finishing
Press and starch each flag. Sew the flowers along the top of the bunting – one between each pair of flags and one at each end.

Wash Cloth

This cloth is just for the pure joy of crochet and anyone with a true passion for crocheting will love making it. What better way to wash your face or the dishes than with a flower! When choosing the yarn, a cotton is best in any thickness, but avoid using mercerised cotton because this is less absorbent.

Skills needed:

- **Treble**
- **Slip stitch**
- **Double treble**
- **Double crochet**
- **Working into a ring**
- **Joining rounds with a slip stitch**
- **Working into a chain space**
- **Decreasing**
- **Creating a square**
- **Joining a new yarn**

YARN

Debbie Bliss Cotton DK, 100% cotton DK (light worsted) yarn, approx 84m (92yd) per 50g (1¾oz) ball

1 ball each of:
58 Fuchsia (deep pink) (A)
02 Ecru (off white) (B)
68 Cloud (pale grey) (C)

HOOK AND EQUIPMENT

3.5mm (US size E/4) crochet hook
Yarn sewing needle

TENSION

Flower centre (Rounds 1–3) measures 9cm (3½in) in diameter, using a 3.5mm (US size E/4) hook and A.

MEASUREMENTS

Finished wash cloth measures 22cm (8¾in) square.

ABBREVIATIONS

See page 27.

SPECIAL ABBREVIATIONS

tr3tog (treble 3 stitches together): [yrh, insert hook in sp, yrh, pull yarn through, yrh, pull through first 2 loops on hook] 3 times in same sp, yrh, pull through all 4 loops on hook

1dtr-1trtog (double treble and treble together): yrh twice, insert hook in sp, yrh, pull yarn through, [yrh, pull through first 2 loops on hook] twice, yrh, insert hook in next sp, yrh, pull yarn through, yrh, pull through first 2 loops on hook, yrh, pull through all 3 loops on hook

1tr-1dtr-1trtog (treble, double treble and treble together): yrh, insert hook in sp, yrh, pull yarn through, yrh, pull through first 2 loops on hook, yrh twice, insert hook in next sp, yrh, pull yarn through, [yrh, pull yarn through first 2 loops on hook] twice, yrh, insert hook in sp, yrh, pull yarn through, yrh, pull through first 2 loops on hook, yrh, pull through all 4 loops on hook

Wash cloth

Using A, make 5ch, join with a ss in first ch to form a ring.

Round 1 (RS): 4ch (counts as 1tr and 1ch), [1tr in ring, 1ch] 7 times, join with a ss in 3rd of first 4-ch. Cont in rounds with RS always facing.

Round 2: 3ch (counts as 1tr), 2tr in same place as last ss, [miss 1 ch, 1ch, 3tr in next tr] 7 times, 1ch, join with a ss in top of first 3-ch. (8 tr-groups)

Round 3: 1ss in each of first 2 tr, 1ss in next ch sp, 4ch (counts as 1tr and 1ch) , [1tr, 1ch, 1tr, 1ch, 1tr] in same sp, *[1tr, 1ch] 3 times in next ch sp, 1tr in same sp; rep from * 6 times more, join with a ss in 3rd of first 4-ch. (8 shell groups) Fasten off A.

Round 4: Join B with a ss in 3rd 1-ch sp of any shell group, 2ch, tr2tog over next sp between 2 shells and next 1-ch sp (between first 2 tr), *3ch, 1ss in next 1-ch sp, 3ch, tr3tog over next 1-ch sp of same shell, next sp between 2 shells and first 1-ch sp of next shell; rep from * 6 times more, 3ch, ss in next ch sp, 3ch, join with a ss in top of first tr2tog.

Round 5: 5ch (counts as 1tr and 2ch), [1tr, 2ch] 3 times (working in top of same tr-2tog), 1tr in same place, *[1tr, 2ch] 4 times in top of next tr-3tog, 1tr in same place; rep from * 6 times more, join with a ss in 3rd of first 5-ch. (8 tr-groups) Fasten off B.

Round 6: Join C in 4th 2-ch sp of any tr-group, 3ch, 1dtr-1trtog over next sp between tr groups and next 2-ch sp (between first 2 tr of next tr group), *5ch, 1dc in next 2-ch sp, 1ch, 1dc in next 2-ch sp, 2ch, tr3tog over next 2-ch sp, next sp between tr groups and next 2-ch sp (between first 2 tr of next tr group), 2ch, 1dc in next 2-ch sp, 1ch, 1dc in next 2-ch sp, 5ch**, 1tr-1dtr-1trtog over next 2 ch, next sp between tr group and next 2-ch sp (between first 2 tr of next tr group); rep from * 3 times more, but ending last rep at **, join with a ss in first dtr.

Round 7: 3ch, [2tr, 2ch, 3tr] in same place as last ss (top of dtr/tr corner group), *3tr in next 5-ch sp, 1tr in next 1-ch sp, 3tr in each of next two 2-ch sps, 1tr in next 1-ch sp, 3tr in next 5-ch sp, [3tr, 2ch, 3tr] in top of next tr/dtr/tr group (corner); rep from * twice more, 3tr in next 5-ch sp, 1tr in next 1-ch sp, 3tr in each of next two 2-ch sps, 1tr in next 1-ch sp, 3tr in next 5-ch sp, join with a ss in top of first 3-ch.

Round 8: 1ss in each of next 2 tr, 1ss in next 2-ch sp corner, 3ch, [2tr, 2ch, 3tr] in same sp, *3tr in next sp between tr groups, [2tr in next sp between tr groups] twice, 3tr in next sp between tr groups, [2tr in next sp between tr groups] twice, 3tr in next sp between tr groups**, [3tr, 2ch, 3tr] in next 2-ch sp corner; rep from * 3 times more, but ending last rep at **, join with a ss in top of first 3-ch.

Round 9: 1ss in each of next 2 tr, 1ss in next 2-ch sp corner, 3ch, [2tr, 2ch, 3tr] in same ch sp, *[3tr in next sp between tr groups] twice, 2tr in next sp between tr groups, [3tr in next sp between tr groups] twice, 2tr in next sp between tr groups, [3tr in next sp between tr groups] twice**, [3tr, 2ch, 3ch] in next 2-ch sp corner; rep from * 3 times more, but ending last rep at **, join with a ss in top of first 3-ch.

Round 10: 1ss in each of next 2 tr, 1ss in next 2-ch sp corner, 3ch, [2tr, 2ch, 3tr] in same ch sp, [3tr in next sp between tr groups] twice, [2tr in next sp between tr groups] twice, 3tr in next sp between tr groups, [2tr in next sp between tr groups] twice, [3tr in next sp between tr groups] twice**, [3tr, 2ch, 3tr] in next 2-ch sp corner; rep from * 3 times more, but ending last rep at **, join with a ss in top of first 3-ch. Fasten off.

Making up and finishing

Sew in ends. Pin and block cloth to shape.

Camellia Blanket

This is a light, beautiful blanket that will cheer up your room at any time of year, but the colours evoke the delicate pinks and pale silver colours of summer.

Skills needed:
- **Double crochet**
- **Treble**
- **Slip stitch**
- **Working into a ring**
- **Joining rounds with a slip stitch**
- **Working into a chain space**
- **Creating a square**
- **Joining a new yarn**
- **Double crochet seam**

YARN
Inner flowers
Debbie Bliss Cashmerino Aran, 55% merino wool, 33% microfibre, 12% cashmere Aran (worsted) yarn, approx 90m (98yd) per 50g (1¾oz) ball
  3 balls each of:
  019 Lilac (A)
  026 Pink (B)
Debbie Bliss Rialto DK, 100% extra-fine merino DK (light worsted) yarn, approx 105m (115yd) per 50g (1¾oz) ball
  3 balls of 88 Apricot (peach) (C)

Leaf
Debbie Bliss Rialto DK, 100% extra-fine merino DK (light worsted) yarn, approx 105m (115yd) per 50g (1¾oz) ball
  5 balls of 59 Willow (green) (D)

One-colour squares
Debbie Bliss Cashmerino Aran, 55% merino wool, 33% microfibre, 12% cashmere Aran (worsted) yarn, approx 90m (98yd) per 50g (1¾oz) ball
  32 balls of 027 Silver Grey (MC)

HOOK AND EQUIPMENT
4.5mm (US size G/6) crochet hook
Yarn sewing needle

TENSION
Tension is not critical on this project.

MEASUREMENTS
Finished blanket measures approx 170 x 125cm (67 x 49in).

ABBREVIATIONS
See page 27.

COLOUR COMBINATIONS
Make a total of 143 squares, 72 flower squares and 71 single colour squares
Centre flower A (make 25)
Centre flower B (make 24)
Centre flower C (make 23)

Flower square
Using A, B or C, 5ch, join with a ss to form a ring.
Round 1: *1dc, 1tr, 1dc into ring; rep from * 3 more times. (4 petals)
Round 2: *2ch, from WS ss in base of 2nd dc of next petal (pick up 2 loops); rep from * 3 more times, slip last stitch into first ss. (4 loops)
Round 3: *4tr in next 2-ch sp (at back), ss in same ch sp; rep from * 3 more times.
Fasten off.
Cont working with same colour. Work into back of petals, picking up two loops. Join yarn at base of highest point of previous round.
Round 4: *3ch, ss in middle of base of the next petal; rep from * 3 more times, slip last st into joining st.
Round 5: *8tr in next 3-ch sp, ss in same 3-ch sp; rep from * 3 more times, slip last st into joining st.
Fasten off.
Change to D. Working into back of petals and picking up two loops as follows, join yarn in middle of base of petal (next 8-tr) of previous round.
Round 6: *3ch, ss in middle of base of the next petal; rep from * 3 more times, slip last st into joining st.

Round 7: *10tr in 3-ch sp, ss in same 3-ch sp; rep from * 3 more times.
Fasten off.
Change to MC.
Working into stitches at top (not at back), join yarn in top of centre tr of one leaf.

Round 8: 4ch (counts as 1tr, 1ch), *3tr in next sp between leaves, 1ch, 3tr, 2ch, 3tr in top of 5th tr of next leaf, 1ch; rep from * twice more. 3tr, 1ch in sp between next leaves, 1ch, 3tr, 2ch, 2tr in same st as start of round, ss in ch sp made from first 4-ch.

Round 9: 3ch, 2tr in same ch sp, 1ch, 3tr in next ch sp, *1ch, 3tr, 2ch, 3tr in next ch sp, 1ch, 3tr in next ch sp, 1ch, 3tr in next ch sp; rep from * twice more. 1ch, 3tr, 2ch, 3tr in next ch sp, 1ch, ss in top of first 3-ch.

Round 10: 1ch, 1dc in each of next 3 sts, 1dc in next ch sp, 1dc in each of next 3 sts, 1dc in next ch sp, *1dc in each of next 3 sts, 2dc in next ch sp, 1dc in each of next 3 sts, 1dc in next ch sp, 1dc in each of next 3 sts, 1dc in next ch sp, 1dc in each of next 3 sts, 1dc in next ch sp; rep from * twice more. 1dc in each of next 3 sts, 2dc in next ch sp, 1dc in each of next 3 sts, 1dc in next ch sp, ss in first dc.
Fasten off.

One-colour squares

Using MC, make 4ch, join with a ss to form a ring.

Round 1: 5ch (counts as 1tr and 2ch), *3tr into ring, 2ch; rep from * twice more, 2tr into ring, ss in 3rd of 5-ch.

Round 2: Ss in next ch sp, 5ch (counts as 1tr and 2ch), 3tr in same sp, *1ch, [3tr, 2ch, 3tr] in next ch sp; rep from * twice more, 1ch, miss 3 sts, 2tr in same sp as 5-ch from previous round, ss in 3rd of 5-ch.

Round 3: Ss in next ch sp, 5ch (counts as 1tr and 2ch), 3tr in same sp, *1ch, miss 3 tr, 3tr in next ch sp, 1ch, miss 3 tr**, [3tr, 2ch, 3tr] in next sp; rep from * twice more and then from * to ** once more, 2tr in same sp as 5-ch, ss in 3rd of 5-ch.

Round 4: Ss in next ch sp, 5ch (counts as 1tr and 2ch), 3tr in same sp, *[1ch, miss 3 tr; 3tr in next ch sp] twice, 1ch, miss 3 tr**, [3tr, 2ch, 3tr] in next ch sp; rep from * twice more and from * to ** once more, 2tr in same sp as 5-ch, ss in 3rd of 5-ch.

Round 5: 1ch, 1dc in same st, 2dc in next ch sp, 1dc in each of next 3 sts, 1dc in next ch sp, 1dc in each of next 3 sts, 1dc in next ch sp, 1dc in each of next 3 sts, 1dc in next ch sp, 1dc in each of next 3 sts, *2dc in next ch sp, 1dc in each of next 3 sts, 1dc in next ch sp, 1dc in each of next 3 sts, 1dc in next ch sp, 1dc in each of next 3 sts, 1dc in next ch sp, 1dc in each of next 3 sts; rep from * once more. 2dc in next ch sp, 1dc in each of next 3 sts, 1dc in next ch sp, 1dc in each of next 3 sts, 1dc in next ch sp, 1dc in each of next 3 sts, 1dc in next ch sp, 1dc in each of next 2 sts, ss in top of first dc.
Fasten off.

Making up and finishing

The blanket is 11 squares wide by 13 squares long, with alternating flower squares and one-colour squares. Place different-coloured flowers at random over the blanket and then join the squares using a double crochet seam.

For the edging

Join in MC and make 1dc in each st along each edge, making 5dc in each of 4 corner stitches.
Fasten off. Sew in ends.

Tip

Sew in ends after completing each square, to avoid having to do them all at the end.

Crown-edged Cushion Cover

Skills needed:
- **Treble**
- **Double crochet**
- **Slip stitch**
- **Working into a ring**
- **Joining rounds with a slip stitch**
- **Working into a chain space**
- **Creating a square**
- **Joining a new yarn**
- **Making a cluster**
- **Making a picot**
- **Double crochet seam**

This is a nice easy project, but I just love making this traditional square using more contemporary colours.

YARN
Rooster Almerino DK, 50% baby alpaca, 50% merino wool DK (light worsted) yarn, approx 112.5m (123yd) per 50g (1¾oz) ball

2 balls each of:
211 Brighton Rock (pink) (A)
214 Damson (dark purple) (E)
1 ball each of:
216 Pier (pale green) (B)
201 Cornish (off white) (C)
218 Starfish (orange) (D)
3 balls of 215 Lilac Sky (pale lilac) (F)

HOOK AND EQUIPMENT
4mm (US size G/6) crochet hook
Yarn sewing needle
40cm (16in) square cushion pad

TENSION
13 sts (approx 4½ 3-tr shells) x 7 rows over a 10cm (4in) square, working shell pattern using a 4mm (US size G/6) hook.

MEASUREMENTS
Finished cushion cover fits a 40cm (16in) square cushion pad.

ABBREVIATIONS
See page 27.

SPECIAL ABBREVIATION
2trCL picot (2-treble cluster picot): [yrh, insert hook in st (or sp), yrh, pull yarn through, yrh, pull yarn through first 2 loops on hook] twice in same st (or sp), yrh, pull yarn through all 3 loops on hook, 3ch, insert hook from right to left through the top 3 loops of 2-trCL just made (4 loops on hook), yrh, pull yarn through all 4 loops on hook

Front
(make 1)
Using A, 4ch, join with a ss in first ch to form a ring.
Round 1 (RS): 3ch (counts as first tr), 2tr in ring, 2ch, *3tr in ring, 2ch; rep from * twice more, join with a ss in top of first 3-ch.
Fasten off A.
Cont in rounds with RS always facing.
Round 2: Join B with a ss in any 2-ch sp, 3ch, 4tr in same sp, 1tr in centre st of next 3-tr group, *5tr in next 2-ch sp, 1tr in centre st of next 3-tr group; rep from * twice more, join with a ss in top of first 3-ch.
Fasten off B.
Round 3: Join C with a ss in centre st of any 5-tr group, 3ch, 5tr in same st, miss 2 tr, 3tr in next tr (centre of side edge), *6tr in centre st of next 5-tr group, miss 2 tr, 3tr in next tr; rep from * twice more, join with a ss in top of first 3-ch.
Fasten off C.
Round 4: Join D with a ss in sp between 3rd and 4th tr of any 6-tr group, 3ch, 5tr in same sp, [3tr in next sp between next two 3-tr

groups] twice, *6tr in sp between 3rd and 4th tr of next 6-tr group, 3tr in each of next 2 sps; rep from * twice more, join with a ss in top of first 3-ch.
Fasten off D.

Round 5: Join E (main colour) with a ss in sp between 3rd and 4th tr of any 6-tr group, 3ch, 5tr in same sp, [3tr in next sp] 3 times, *6tr in sp between 3rd and 4th tr of next 6-tr group, [3tr in next sp] 3 times; rep from * twice more, join with a ss in top of first 3-ch. Do not fasten off, but cont with E to complete front.

Round 6: 1ss in each of next 2 tr, 1ss in sp between 3rd and 4th tr of this 6-tr group, 3ch, 5tr in same sp, 3tr in each sp between 3-tr groups to next 6-tr corner group, *6tr in sp between 3rd and 4th tr of next 6-tr group, 3tr in each sp to next 6-tr corner group; rep from * twice more, join with a ss in top of first 3-ch.

Rounds 7–17: Rep Round 6 eleven times (increasing number of 3-tr groups between corners in each round), work now measures approx 40cm (16in) square.
Fasten off.

Edging:
Round 1: With RS facing and using A, join yarn in sp between 3rd and 4th tr of any 6-tr corner group, 1ch, 2dc in same place, 1dc in each tr to next 6-tr group, *1tr in each of first 3 tr of 6-tr group, [2dc, 1ch, 2dc] in sp between 3rd and 4th tr of this 6-tr group, 1dc in each tr to next 6-tr corner group; rep from * twice more, 2dc in same corner as first 2-dc of round, 1ch, join with a ss in first dc of round.
Fasten off.

Back
(make 1)
Using F, make 4ch, join with ss in first ch to form a ring.
Round 1 (RS): As Round 1 of front. Cont in rounds with RS always facing.

Round 2: 1ss in each of next 2 tr, 1ss in next 2-ch sp, 3ch (counts as first tr), 4tr in same sp, 1tr in centre st of next 3-tr group, *5tr in next 2-ch sp, 1tr in centre st of next 3-tr group; rep from * twice more, join with a ss in top of first 3-ch.

Round 3: 1ss in each of next 2 tr, 3ch, 5tr in same place as last ss (centre st of 5-tr group), miss 2 tr, 3tr in next tr (centre of side edge), *6tr in centre st of next 5-tr group, miss 2 tr, 3tr in next tr; rep from * twice more, join with a ss in top of first 3-ch.

Round 4: 1ss in each of next 2 tr, 1ss in sp between 3rd and 4th tr of this 6-tr corner group, 3ch, 5tr in same sp, 3tr in each sp between 3-tr groups to next 6-tr corner group, *6tr in sp between 3rd and 4th tr of next 6-tr group, 3tr in each sp between 3-tr groups to next 6-tr corner group; rep from * to end, join with a ss in top of first 3-ch.
Rep Round 4 until same number of rounds have been worked as on front.
Fasten off.

Edging:
Round 1: With RS facing and using A, work as for front.
Fasten off.

Making up and finishing
Join the front and back with WS together and working all sts through both pieces.
Join A with a ss in any 1-ch sp corner, 1ch, [2dc, 1ch, 2dc] in same sp, 1dc in each st to next 1-ch sp corner, *[2dc, 1ch, 2dc] in next 1-ch sp, 1dc in each st to next 1-ch sp corner; rep from * twice more (inserting cushion pad before closing last side), join with a ss in first dc.
Do not fasten off.

For the crown edging
Using A, make 3ch, miss 1 dc, 2trCL picot in next 1-ch sp corner, 3ch, miss 2 dc, 1dc in next dc, *3ch, miss 1 dc, 2trCL picot in next dc, 3ch, miss 1 dc, 1dc in next dc*; rep from * to * to next '2ch, 1ch, 2dc' corner group, **3ch, miss 2 dc, 2trCL picot in 1ch sp corner, 3ch, miss 2 dc, 1dc in next dc**; rep from * to * along each edge and from ** to ** at each corner to end, join with a ss in base of first 3-ch.
Fasten off.

Sweetheart Blanket

A gorgeous cot blanket or sitting-on-the-sofa-blanket. All the squares are exactly the same heart design, but made in a variety of pretty colours.

Skills needed:
- **Double crochet**
- **Working in rows**
- **Intarsia**
- **Double crochet seam**
- **Joining rounds with a slip stitch**

YARN

Rooster Almerino DK, 50% baby alpaca, 50% merino wool DK (light worsted) yarn, approx 113m (124yd) per 50g (1¾oz) ball

10 balls of 201 Cornish (off white) (MC)

1 ball each of:

218 Starfish (orange)

219 Sandcastle (pale yellow)

205 Glace (pale blue)

203 Strawberry Cream (pale pink)

211 Brighton Rock (pink)

204 Grape (purple)

216 Pier (pale green)

215 Lilac Sky (pale lilac)

217 Beach (turquoise) (CC)

HOOK AND EQUIPMENT

3mm (US size D/3) crochet hook
Yarn sewing needle

TENSION

21 rows x 21 sts over a 10cm (4in) square, working double crochet using a 3mm (D/3) hook.

MEASUREMENTS

Finished blanket measures approx 92 x 76.5cm (36 x 30½in).

Heart motif chart

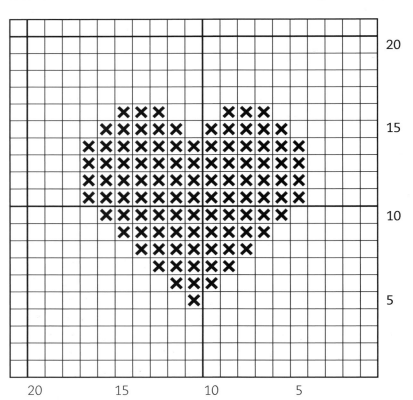

ABBREVIATIONS

See page 27.

Squares

(make 63, 7 of each colour heart)
Using MC, make 22ch.
Row 1 (RS): 1dc in 2nd ch from hook, 1dc in each ch to end. (21 dc)
Row 2: 1ch (does not count as a st), 1dc in each dc to end.
Rows 3–4: Rep Row 2.

Cont in dc throughout, following chart for Rows 5–16 to work the heart motif, and using one small ball of MC on each side of motif. Read the chart from bottom up, working odd-number rows from right to left and even-number rows from left to right.

Using MC only, work 5 more rows in dc. Fasten off.

Making up and finishing

Lay the squares out on a flat surface in strips of 7 squares across by 9 squares down, so different colour hearts are arranged evenly across the blanket. Using A and with WS together, join the rows into strips using a double crochet seam, then join the strips together vertically.

For the edging

Round 1: Join A in top right-hand corner of blanket, make 1dc in same corner, *1dc in each st along edge to next corner, 2dc in corner sts; rep from * twice more, 1dc in each st along edge to last corner, 1dc in corner st, ss in first dc.

Round 2: 1ch, 1dc in each st along edge to next corner, 2dc in corner sts; rep from * twice more, 1dc in each st along edge to next corner, ss in first 1-ch.

Round 3: 3ch, 1tr in each st along edge to next corner, 2tr in corner sts; rep from * twice more, 1tr in each st along edge to next corner, ending 1tr in same space as first 3-ch, ss in top of first 3-ch. Fasten off.

Sew in ends on WS. Block the blanket to size.

Baby Cloths

These are handy and pretty little cloths to take around in your baby bag – so lovely you'll put everyone else's muslin cloths to shame. I adapted these traditional square patterns from vintage patterns found in my mother's craft drawer that were due for a well-earned airing.

Skills needed:

- **Treble**
- **Slip stitch**
- **Double crochet**
- **Double treble**
- **Working into a ring**
- **Joining rounds with a slip stitch**
- **Working into a chain space**
- **Creating a square**
- **Joining a new yarn**
- **Working in rows**
- **Decreasing**
- **Increasing**

YARN

Traditional square
Rowan Handknit Cotton DK, 100% cotton, DK (light worsted) yarn, approx 85m (93yd) per 50g (1¾oz) ball
1 ball each of:
351 Cassis (pink) (A)
239 Ice Water (light blue) (B)
346 Atlantic (mid-blue) (C)

Wave cloth
Rowan Handknit Cotton DK, 100% cotton, DK (light worsted) yarn, approx 85m (93yd) per 50g (1¾oz) ball
1 ball each of:
334 Delphinium (lilac) (A)
352 Sea Foam (turquoise) (B)
239 Ice Water (light blue) (D)
346 Atlantic (mid-blue) (F)
Debbie Bliss Cotton DK, 100% cotton DK (light worsted) yarn, approx 84m (92yd) per 50g (1¾oz) ball
1 ball each of:
58 Fuchsia (bright pink) (C)
75 English Mustard (yellow) (E)

HOOKS AND EQUIPMENT
4.5mm (US size G/6) and 4mm (US size F/5) crochet hooks
Yarn sewing needle

TENSION
Tension is not critical on this project.

MEASUREMENTS
Traditional square measures 22.5cm (9in) square
Wave cloth measures 22.5cm (9in) square

ABBREVIATIONS
See page 27.

Traditional square

Using a 4.5mm (US size G/6) hook and A, make 4ch, join with a ss to form a ring.

Round 1: 3ch (counts as first tr), 2tr into ring, 2ch, *3tr into ring, 2ch; rep from * twice more; join with a ss in first 3-ch.
Join B.

Round 2: Ss in first 2-ch sp, 3ch, [1tr, 2ch, 3tr] in same ch sp, 1ch; *[3tr, 2ch, 3tr] in next ch sp (corner), 1ch; rep from * twice more, 1tr in next ch sp, join with a ss. (4 corners)
Join C.

Round 3: Ss in first 2-ch sp, 3ch, [1tr, 2ch, 3tr] in same sp, 1ch, 3tr in next ch sp, 1ch, *[3tr, 2ch, 3tr] in next corner sp, 1ch, 3tr in next ch sp, 1ch; rep from * twice more, 1tr in next ch sp, join with a ss. Alternate colours as set in each following round.

Rounds 4–8: Ss in first 2-ch sp, 3ch, [1tr, 2ch, 3tr] in same ch sp, 1ch, [3tr in next ch sp, 1ch] in each ch sp to corner, [3tr, 2ch, 3tr] in corner sp; rep from * twice more, 1tr in next ch sp, join with a ss.
Fasten off.

Wave cloth

Using a 4mm (US size F/5) hook and A, make 33ch.

Row 1: 1tr in 2nd ch from hook, 1tr in next ch, *1tr in each of next 3 ch, tr3tog over next 3 sts, 1tr in each of next 3-ch, 3tr in next ch; rep from * ending last rep with 2tr in last ch.
Break yarn.

Row 2: Join B in first st, 2ch, 1tr in first st, *1tr in each of next 3 sts, tr3tog over next 3 sts, 1tr in each of next 3 sts, 3tr in next st; rep from * ending last rep with 2tr in last ch.

Fasten off.

Rows 3–15: Repeat Row 2, changing colour for each row as follows: A, C, A, D, A, E, A, F, A, C, A, B, A.
Fasten off.

Making up and finishing

Sew in ends on WS. Block the cloths to size.

Skills needed:

- **Treble**
- **Slip stitch**
- **Double crochet**
- **Working into a ring**
- **Joining rounds with a slip stitch**
- **Working in rounds**
- **Working into a chain space**
- **Joining a new yarn**
- **Loop stitch**
- **Making an oversewn seam**

Hexagon Flower Throw

Although it looks complicated, this gorgeous throw actually involves simple techniques – it just takes a little time to complete, depending on how large you would like your throw to be.

YARN

Rooster Almerino DK, 50% baby alpaca, 50% merino wool DK (light worsted) yarn, approx 113m (124yd) per 50g (1¾oz) ball

15 balls of 201 Cornish (off white) (A)

4 balls each of:

208 Ocean (blue-green) (B)

205 Glace (pale blue) (C)

3 balls each of:

216 Pier (pale green) (D)

218 Starfish (orange) (E)

219 Sandcastle (pale yellow) (F)

2 balls each of 203 Strawberry Cream (pale pink) (G)

204 Grape (purple) (H)

215 Lilac Sky (pale lilac) (I)

211 Brighton Rock (pink) (J)

210 Custard (yellow) (K)

1 ball of 207 Gooseberry (green) (L)

HOOK AND EQUIPMENT

4mm (US size G/6) crochet hook

Yarn sewing needle

TENSION

Each hexagon measures approx 13cm (5in) from side to side and 15cm (6in) from point to point, using a 4mm (US size G/6) hook.

MEASUREMENTS

Finished throw measures approx 137 x 129.5cm (54 x 51in).

ABBREVIATIONS

See page 27.

SPECIAL ABBREVIATION

1dc loop st (1 double crochet loop stitch): insert hook in 1-ch sp of round before previous round, yrh, pull yarn through drawing it up to extend the loop, yrh, pull yarn through both loops on hook to complete the loop stitch

COLOUR COMBINATIONS

Hexagon 1: colour 1 = D, colour 2 = G, colour 3 = J, colour 4 = A (make 17)

Hexagon 2: colour 1 = E, colour 2 = I, colour 3 = H, colour 4 = A (make 17)

Hexagon 3: colour 1 = E, colour 2 = C, colour 3 = B, colour 4 = A (make 17)

Hexagon 4: colour 1 = B, colour 2 = F, colour 3 = K, colour 4 = A (make 17)

Hexagon 5: colour 1 = J, colour 2 = D, colour 3 = L, colour 4 = A (make 16)

Hexagon 6: colour 1 = F, colour 2 = C, colour 3 = B, colour 4 = A (make 13)

Hexagon 7: colour 1 = K, colour 2 = B, colour 3 = C, colour 4 = A (make 6)

Hexagon 8: colour 1 = E, colour 2 = H, colour 3 = I, colour 4 = A (make 4)

Hexagon 9: colour 1 = B, colour 2 = K, colour 3 = F, colour 4 = A (make 4)

Hexagon 10: colour 1 = E, colour 2 = B, colour 3 = C, colour 4 = A (make 2)

Hexagon 11: colour 1 = G, colour 2 = L, colour 3 = D, colour 4 = A (make 1)

Hexagon

(make 114)

Using colour 1, make 5ch, join with a ss in first ch to form a ring.

Round 1 (RS): 3ch (counts as 1tr), 1tr into ring, 1ch, *2tr into ring, 1ch; rep from * 4 times more, join with a ss in top of first 3-ch. (6 groups)

Fasten off colour 1. Cont in rounds with RS always facing.

Round 2: Join colour 2 with a ss in any 1-ch sp, 3ch, [1tr, 2ch, 2tr] in same sp, 1ch, *[2tr, 2ch, 2tr] in next 1-ch sp, 1ch; rep from * 4 times more, join with a ss in top of first 3-ch.

Round 3: 1ss in top of next tr, 1ss in next 2-ch sp, 3ch, 6tr in same sp, 1ch, *7tr in next 2-ch sp, 1ch; rep from * 4 times more, break off colour 3, but do not fasten off, join in colour 4 with a ss in top of first 3-ch.

Round 4: 1ch, 1dc in same place as last ss, 1dc in each of next 6 tr, 1dc loop st in next 1-ch sp of Round 2, *1dc in each of next 7 tr, 1dc loop st in next 1-ch sp of Round 2; rep from * 4 times more, break off colour 3, but do not fasten off, join colour 4 with a ss in first dc.

Round 5: 3ch, 1tr in each of next 2 sts, 3tr in next st, 1tr in each of next 3 sts, *miss next dc loop st, 1tr in each of next 3 sts, 3tr in next st, 1tr in each of next 3 sts; rep from * 4 times more, join with a ss in top of first 3-ch.

Round 6: 1ch, 1dc in same place as last ss, 1dc in each of next 3 tr, *3dc in next tr (centre st of 3-tr group – corner), 1dc in each of next 8 tr; rep from * 4 times more, 3dc in next tr (centre tr of 3-tr group – corner), 1dc in each of next 4 dc, join with a ss in first dc. Fasten off.

Making up and finishing

Lay hexagons out on a flat surface to evenly arrange the colours. Using the layout diagram (below) as a guide, alternate hexagons in rows of 9 and then 10, starting the first row with 9 hexagons. Sew hexagons together with RS facing using an oversewn seam.

For the edging

With RS facing, join A with a ss in top right-hand corner hexagon, in any st along straight edge but not in any corner st (outer tip of hexagon), then work 1ch, 1dc in same place as ss, 1dc in each st to first outer tip (corner), 3dc in centre st of tip (centre st of a 3-dc group), *1dc in each st to next corner outer tip, 3dc in centre st of next corner outer tip; rep from * to end, join with a ss in first dc. Fasten off.

Hexagon flower throw layout

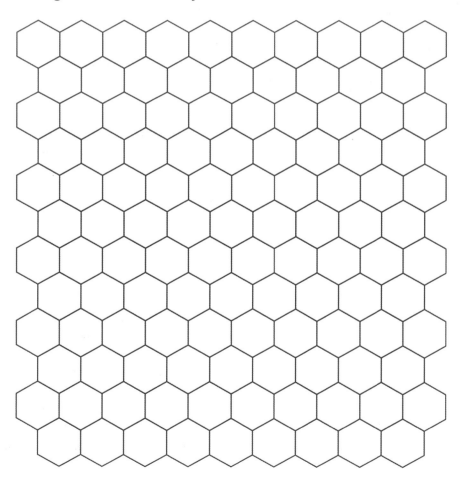

Buggy Blanket

Skills needed:

- **Slip stitch**
- **Double crochet**
- **Treble**
- **Working into a ring**
- **Joining rounds with a slip stitch**
- **Joining a new yarn**
- **Working in rounds**
- **Making a cluster**
- **Working into a chain space**
- **Creating a square**
- **Backstitch**

This is a really colourful and eye-catching blanket for a buggy or a car seat. The first square uses slightly more complex crochet to create the three-dimensional flowers – but once you've mastered it, you'll just repeat it until you have enough squares for your blanket.

YARN

Rooster Almerino DK, 50% baby alpaca, 50% merino wool DK (light worsted) yarn, approx 113m (124yd) per 50g (1¾oz) ball

2 balls each of:
210 Custard (yellow) (A)
211 Brighton Rock (pink) (B)
203 Strawberry Cream (pale pink) (C)
208 Ocean (blue-green) (D),
220 Lighthouse (red) (E)
207 Gooseberry (green) (F)
215 Lilac Sky (pale lilac) (G)
1 ball each of:
218 Starfish (orange) (H)
217 Beach (turquoise) (J)
204 Grape (purple) (K)

HOOK AND EQUIPMENT

5mm (US size H/8) crochet hook
Yarn sewing needle

TENSION

Each square measures 8 x 8cm (3¼ x 3¼in), using a 5mm (US size H/8) hook.

MEASUREMENTS

Finished throw measures approx 48 x 64cm (19½ x 26in).

ABBREVIATIONS

See page 27.

SPECIAL ABBREVIATIONS

2trCL (2-treble cluster): [yrh, insert hook in st, yrh, pull yarn through, yrh, pull through first 2 loops on hook] twice in same st, yrh, pull through all 3 loops on hook

3trCL (3-treble cluster): [yrh, insert hook in st, yrh, pull yarn through, yrh, pull through first 2 loops on hook] 3 times in same st, yrh, pull through all 4 loops on hook

COLOUR COMBINATIONS

Make 8 of each colourway.
Square 1: colour 1 = A, colour 2 = B, colour 3 = C, colour 4 = D, colour 5 = J
Square 2: colour 1 = E, colour 2 = H, colour 3 = A, colour 4 = F, colour 5 = B
Square 3: colour 1 = A, colour 2 = B, colour 3 = E, colour 4 = F, colour 5 = G
Square 4: colour 1 = A, colour 2 = D, colour 3 = J, colour 4 = F, colour 5 = E
Square 5: colour 1 = A, colour 2 = E, colour 3 = C, colour 4 = F, colour 5 = A
Square 6: colour 1 = A, colour 2 = J, colour 3 = G, colour 4 = F, colour 5 = C

Square

(make 48)

Using colour 1, make 4ch and join with a ss in first ch to form a ring.

Round 1 (RS): 1ch, 8dc into ring, break off colour 1, join colour 2 with a ss in first dc.

Cont in rounds with RS always facing.

Round 2: 3ch, 1tr in same place as last ss (counts as first 2trCL), 2ch, *2trCL in next st, 2ch; rep from * to end, join with a ss in first tr. (8 clusters)

Fasten off colour 2.

Round 3: Join colour 3 with a ss in any 2-ch sp, *3ch, [3trCL, 4ch, 1ss] in same sp (1 petal made), 1dc in top of next 2-trCL, 1ss in next 2-ch sp; rep from * working last ss in same sp as first petal. (8 petals)

Fasten off colour 3.

Round 4: Join colour 4 with a ss in top of any dc between petals, 1ch, 1dc in same place as ss, *keeping petal at front of work, 3ch, 1dc in next dc (between next 2 petals), 2ch, 1dc in next dc; rep from * to end, join with a ss in first dc. (8 ch sps)

Do not fasten off, but cont with colour 4.

Round 5: 1ss in first 3-ch sp, 3ch (counts as 1tr), [2tr, 2ch, 3tr] in same sp (corner), *1ch, 2tr in next 2-ch sp, 1ch, [3tr, 2ch, 3tr] in next 3-ch sp (corner); rep from * twice more, *1ch, 2tr in last 2-ch sp, 1ch, join with a ss in top of first 3-ch.

Fasten off colour 4.

Round 6: Join colour 5 with a ss in any 2-ch sp corner, 3ch (counts as 1tr), [2tr, 2ch, 3tr] in same sp (corner), 3tr in each of next two 1-ch sps, *[3tr, 2ch, 3tr] in 2-ch sp corner, 3tr in each of next two 1-ch sps; rep from * to end, join with a ss in top of first 3-ch.

Fasten off.

Making up and finishing

Sew in the ends. Arrange the squares in 8 horizontal rows of 6 squares each, using all 6 colourways in each row but arranging them in random order. With WS together, join the squares together in rows of 6 using backstitch, and then join the 8 rows together in the same way.

For the edging

Join J with a ss in any corner sp, 1ch, 3dc in same sp, *1dc in each st of first square to corner ch sp of first seam, 1dc in ch sp (at end of first square), [1dc in next ch sp (of next square), 1dc in each st to corner ch sp of same square, 1dc in ch sp] rep to next corner of blanket, 2dc in same corner sp; rep from * to end, join with a ss in first dc.

Fasten off.

Oven Cloths

Skills needed:
- **Double crochet**
- **Treble**
- **Slip stitch**
- **Working into a ring**
- **Joining rounds with a slip stitch**
- **Working into a chain space**
- **Creating a square**
- **Joining a new yarn**
- **Making a cluster**
- **Adding a lining**

These are such a pretty addition to anyone's kitchen. I much prefer them to oven gloves – I usually need to get into the oven in a hurry and don't have time to put on gloves. I can't believe I haven't designed something like these before!

YARN

Cloth 1

Rooster Almerino DK, 50% baby alpaca, 50% merino wool DK (light worsted) yarn, approx 113m (124yd) per 50g (1¾oz) ball
1 ball each of:
210 Custard (yellow) (A)
211 Brighton Rock (pink) (B)
203 Strawberry Cream (pale pink) (C),
208 Ocean (blue-green) (D)
205 Glace (pale blue) (E)
217 Beach (turquoise) (F)

Cloth 2

Rooster Almerino DK, 50% baby alpaca, 50% merino wool DK (light worsted) yarn, approx 113m (124yd) per 50g (1¾oz) ball
1 ball each of:
216 Pier (A)
203 Strawberry Cream (pale pink) (B)
211 Brighton Rock (pink) (C)
219 Sandcastle (pale yellow) (E)
210 Custard (yellow) (F)
Debbie Bliss Rialto DK, 100% extra-fine merino DK (light worsted) yarn, approx 105m (115yd) per 50g (1¾oz) ball
1 ball of 312 Olive (green) (D)

HOOK AND EQUIPMENT

4mm (US size G/6) crochet hook
30 x 40cm (12 x 16in) of lining fabric, for each cloth
22.5cm (9in) square of heat-resistant cloth, for each cloth
Sewing needle and thread to match

TENSION

First 5 rounds of cloth measure 9.5cm (3¾in) square using a 4mm (US size G/6) hook.

MEASUREMENTS

Each cloth measures 21.5cm (8½in) square.

ABBREVIATIONS

See page 27.

SPECIAL ABBREVIATIONS

2trCL (2-treble cluster): [yrh, insert hook in st (or sp), yrh, pull yarn through, yrh, pull yarn through first 2 loops on hook] twice in same st, yrh, pull through all 3 loops on hook
3trCL (3-treble cluster): [yrh, insert hook in st (or sp), yrh, pull yarn through, yrh, pull yarn through first 2 loops on hook] 3 times in same st, yrh, pull yarn through all 4 loops on hook

Cloth

Using A, make 4ch, join with a ss in first ch to form a ring.
Round 1 (RS): 1ch, 8dc into ring, break off A, join in B with a ss in first dc.
Cont in rounds with RS always facing.
Round 2: 3ch, 1tr in same place as last ss (3ch and 1tr count as first 2trCL), 2ch, *2trCL in next dc, 2ch; rep from * to end, join with a ss in first tr. (8 clusters)
Fasten off B.
Round 3: Join C with a ss in any 2-ch sp, 3ch, [3trCL, 3ch, 1ss] in same sp as last ss (1 petal made), 1dc in top of next 2-trCL, *[1ss, 3ch, 3trCL, 4ch, 1ss] in next 2-ch sp, 1dc in top of next 2-trCL; rep from * to end, join with a ss in same sp as first petal. (8 petals)
Fasten off C.
Round 4: Join D with a ss in any dc between petals, 1ch, 1dc in same st, *keeping petal at front of work, 3ch, 1dc in next dc (between petals), 2ch, 1dc in next dc; rep from * to end, join with a ss in first dc. (8 ch sps)
Do not fasten off, but cont with D for next round.

Round 5: 1ss in first 3-ch sp, 3ch (counts as 1tr), [2tr, 2ch, 3tr] in same sp (corner), *1ch, 2tr in next 2-ch sp, 1ch, [3tr, 2ch, 3tr] in next 3-ch sp (corner); rep from * to last 2-ch sp, 1ch, 2tr in last 2-ch sp, 1ch, join with a ss in top of first 3-ch. Fasten off D.

Round 6: Join E in any 2-ch sp corner, 3ch (counts as 1tr), [2tr, 2ch, 3tr] in same sp (corner), 3tr in each of next two 1-ch sps, *[3tr, 2ch, 3tr] in next 2-ch sp corner, 3tr in each of next two 1-ch sps; rep from * to end, join with a ss in top of first 3-ch. Fasten off E.

Round 7: Join F in any 2-ch sp corner, 3ch (counts as 1tr), [2tr, 2ch, 3tr] in same sp (corner), [3tr in sp between next two 3-tr groups] 3 times, *[3tr, 2ch, 3tr] in next 2-ch sp corner, [3tr in sp between next two 3-tr groups] 3 times; rep from * to end, join with a ss in top of first 3-ch. Do not fasten off, but cont with F to complete cloth.

Round 8: 1ss in each of next 2 tr, 1ss in next 2-ch sp, 3ch (counts as 1tr), [2tr, 2ch, 3tr] in same sp (corner), 3tr in each sp between 3-tr groups to next '3tr, 2ch, 3tr' corner group, *[3tr, 2ch, 3tr] in next 2-ch sp corner, 3tr in each sp between 3-tr groups to next '3tr, 2ch, 3tr' corner group; rep from * to end, join with a ss in top of first 3-ch.

Rounds 9–12: Rep Round 8. Fasten off.

Making up and finishing

Sew in ends. Block and steam.

For the tab
Cut a piece of lining fabric 12 x 21cm (4¾ x 8¼in). Fold in half

lengthways with WS together and press, then open out. Fold both long raw edges to meet at the centre foldline and press. Fold the tab in half again along the first foldline to conceal the long raw edges and then sew together along the open long edge. Fold the tab in half widthways to create a loop and set aside.

For the lining
Cut a piece of lining fabric 1.5cm (⅝in) larger all around than the finished oven cloth and a piece of heat-resistant fabric the same size

as the oven cloth. Fold under and press a hem of 1.5cm (⅝in) along each edge of the lining fabric. Place the heat-resistant fabric on the lining with WS together, slip the raw ends of the tab in between the heat-resistant fabric and the lining in one corner, pin and machine sew around all four sides securing the tab at the same time. Place the heat-resistant side of the lining on the WS of the oven cloth. Pin and oversew around all four edges.

Vintage-style Vase Coaster

Vintage crochet mats are very popular at the moment, so why not make your own? Traditionally mats were made using very fine cotton yarn, but I've used DK-weight cotton for a much quicker project. The pattern is a little intricate, but the stitches are easy.

Skills needed:
- **Treble**
- **Slip stitch**
- **Double crochet**
- **Double treble**
- **Working into a ring**
- **Joining rounds with a slip stitch**
- **Working in rounds**
- **Working into a chain space**
- **Joining a new yarn**

YARN

Mat 1

Rowan Cotton Glacé, 100% cotton DK (light worsted) yarn, approx 115m (125yd) per 50g (1¾oz) ball

1 ball each of:
832 Persimmon (orange) (A)
725 Ecru (off white) (B)
862 Blackcurrant (C)
845 Shell (pale pink) (D)
814 Shoot (green) (E)

Mat 2

Rowan Cotton Glacé, 100% cotton DK (light worsted) yarn, approx 115m (125yd) per 50g (1¾oz) ball

1 ball each of:
861 Rose (A)

845 Shell (pale pink) (B)
862 Blackcurrant (C)
725 Ecru (off white) (D)
833 Ochre (E)

HOOK AND EQUIPMENT
3mm (US size D/3) crochet hook
Yarn sewing needle

TENSION
First 4 rounds of mat pattern measure 13.5cm (5¼in) in diameter, using a 3mm (US size D/3) hook.

MEASUREMENTS
Finished mat measures 28cm (11in) in diameter.

ABBREVIATIONS
See page 27.

Coaster
Using A, make 6ch, join with a ss in first ch to form a ring.

Round 1 (RS): 3ch (counts as 1tr), 2tr into ring, 2ch, [3tr, 2ch] 5 times into ring, join with a ss in top of first 3-ch. Fasten off A.
Cont in rounds with RS always facing.

Round 2: Join B with a ss in any 2-ch sp, 3ch, [2tr, 2ch, 3tr] in same 2-ch sp, 1ch, *[3tr, 2ch, 3tr, 1ch] in next 2-ch sp; rep from * 4 times, join with a ss in top of first 3-ch. Fasten off B.

Round 3: Join C with a ss in any 1-ch sp, 3ch (counts as 1tr), 2tr in same 1-ch sp, 1ch, *[3tr, 2ch, 3tr, 1ch] in next 2-ch sp, 3tr in next 1-ch sp, 1ch; rep from * 4 times, [3tr, 2ch, 3tr, 1ch] in next 2-ch sp, join with a ss in top of first 3-ch. Break off C, but do not fasten off.

Round 4: Join in D, 1ss in next tr (centre st of 3-tr group), 3ch (counts as 1tr), 2tr in same place as ss just worked, 1dc in next 1-ch sp, 1ch, *[1tr, 1ch] 6 times in next 2-ch sp, 1dc in next 1-ch sp**, 3tr in centre st of next 3-tr group, 1dc in next 1-ch sp, 1ch; rep from * ending last rep at **, join with a ss in top of first 3-ch.
Break off D, but do not fasten off.

Round 5: Join in E, 4ch (counts as 1dtr), 1tr in top of first 3-ch in previous round, 1tr in each of next 2 tr, 1dtr in next dc, *4ch, 1dc in 1-ch sp in centre of next 6-tr

Tip

When working on the flower round, make sure that you are always working with the right side facing you.

group, 4ch**, 1dtr in next dc, 1tr in each of next 3 tr, 1dtr in next dc; rep from * ending last rep at **, join with a ss in top of first 4-ch. Do not fasten off.

Round 6: Cont with E, 3ch (counts as 1tr), *1tr in each of next 3 tr, 1tr in next dtr, 7tr in next 4-ch sp, miss next dc, 7tr in next 4-ch sp**, 1tr in next dtr; rep from * ending last rep at **, join with a ss in top of first 3-ch.
Break off E, but do not fasten off.

Round 7: Join in B (or D), 1ch, *miss next 2 tr, [2tr, 2ch, 2tr] in next tr, miss next 2 tr, 1dc in next tr; rep from * omitting dc at end of last rep, join with a ss in top of first tr at beg of round. Do not fasten off.

Round 8: Cont with B (or D), 3ch (counts as 1tr), 1tr in next tr, *[2tr, 2ch, 2tr] in next 2-ch sp, 1tr in each of next 2 tr**, miss next dc, 1tr in each of next 2 tr; rep from * ending last rep at **, join with a ss in top of first 3-ch.
Fasten off B (or D).

Round 9 (flower round): Join A with a ss in any 2-ch sp, 1ch, 1dc in same 2-ch sp, *4ch, form a ring by joining with a ss in first ch of 4-ch just made, [3ch, 1tr into ring, 3ch, 1ss into ring] 5 times (5 petals – 1 flower – made), 1ss in dc at base of flower, 1dc in each of next 8 tr**, 1dc in next 2-ch sp; rep from * ending last rep at **, join with a ss in first dc.
Fasten off.

Making up and finishing

Block, starch and press the coaster.

Hexagon Blanket

This blanket is one of my favourite projects in the book; I love the simplicity, I love the yarn and the colours. Please play with the colours and choose them to suit your colour scheme – but if you always use the same colour for Round 2, it will really make the contrasting colours stand out.

Skills needed:
- **Treble**
- **Double crochet**
- **Slip stitch**
- **Working into a ring**
- **Joining rounds with a slip stitch**
- **Working in rounds**
- **Working into a chain space**
- **Joining a new yarn**
- **Making a cluster**
- **Double crochet seam**

YARN
Debbie Bliss Baby Cashmerino, 55% merino wool, 33% microfibre, 12% cashmere lightweight DK (sportweight) yarn, approx 125m (137yd) per 50g (1¾oz) ball
9 balls of 101 Ecru (off white) (MC)
3 balls each of:
001 Primrose (yellow) (A)
202 Light Blue (B)
059 Mallard (teal blue) (C)
305 Blush (peach) (D)
018 Citrus (pale green) (E)

HOOK AND EQUIPMENT
3mm (US size D/3) crochet hook
Yarn sewing needle

TENSION
Each hexagon measures 9cm (3½in) edge to edge, using a 3mm (US size D/3) hook.

MEASUREMENTS
Finished blanket measures approx 177 x 177cm (46 x 46in).

ABBREVIATIONS
See page 27.

COLOUR COMBINATIONS
Hexagon 1: Centre = A, Round 2 = MC, Rounds 3 and 4 = D (make 37)
Hexagon 2: Centre = B, Round 2 = MC, Rounds 3 and 4 = C (make 37)
Hexagon 3: Centre = C, Round 2 = MC, Rounds 3 and 4 = E (make 37)
Hexagon 4: Centre = D, Round 2 = MC, Rounds 3 and 4 = A (make 38)
Hexagon 5: Centre = E, Round 2 = MC, Rounds 3 and 4 = B (make 38)

SPECIAL ABBREVIATIONS
2trCL (2-treble cluster): [Yrh, insert hook in sp, yrh, pull yarn through work, yrh, pull yarn through first 2 loops on hook] twice in same sp (3 loops now on hook), yrh and pull yarn through all 3 loops on hook to complete 2trCL

3trCL (3-treble cluster): [Yrh, insert hook in sp, yrh, pull yarn through work, yrh, pull yarn through first 2 loops on hook] 3 times in same sp (4 loops now on hook), yrh, pull yarn through all 4 loops on hook to complete the 3trCL

Hexagons

(make 187)

Foundation ring: Using either A, B, C, D or E, make 6ch and join with a ss in first chain to form a ring.

Round 1 (RS): 3ch, 2trCL into ring, 2ch, [3trCL into ring, 2ch] 5 times, join with a ss in 3rd of first 3-ch. (6 clusters)

Fasten off.

Cont in rounds with RS always facing you.

Round 2: Join MC with a ss in any 2-ch sp between any 3-trCL groups from previous round, 3ch, [2trCL, 2ch, 3trCL] in same ch sp, *2ch, [3trCL, 2ch, 3trCL] in next 2-ch sp; rep from * 4 times more, 2ch, join with a ss in 3rd of first 3-ch. (12 clusters)

Fasten off.

Round 3 (hexagon round): Join a contrasting colour from A, B, C, D or E with a ss in 2-ch sp in middle of any '3trCL, 2ch, 3trCL' group, 3ch, [2tr, 2ch, 3tr] in same sp (corner), *3tr in next 2-ch sp, [3tr, 2ch, 3tr] in next ch sp (corner); rep from * 4 times more, 3tr in next ch sp, join with a ss in 3rd of first 3-ch. (6 corners)

Do not fasten off.

Round 4: Cont using same colour, 1ch, 1dc in each of next 2 sts, 2dc in next ch sp (corner), *1dc in each of next 9 sts, 2dc in next ch sp (corner); rep from * 4 times more, 1dc in each of next 6 sts, join with a ss in top of first dc.

Fasten off.

Making up and finishing

Sew in the yarn ends.
Lay the hexagons out on a flat surface to evenly arrange the colours. Using the layout diagram (right) as a guide, alternate hexagons in rows of 12 and then 13, starting the first row with 12 hexagons and ending the last row with 12 hexagons.

Using MC, join the hexagons with a double crochet seam, working with WS together so the seam shows on the RS.

For the edging
With RS facing, join MC in the top left-hand corner in the 2nd of the 2 corner dc at the top of the first hexagon on the first row.

Make 1ch, 3dc in same place as join, 1dc in each dc along each straight edge, 3dc in 2nd of 2 dc at each corner and 1ss in each seam around outer edge, ss in first dc. Fasten off.

Hexagon blanket layout

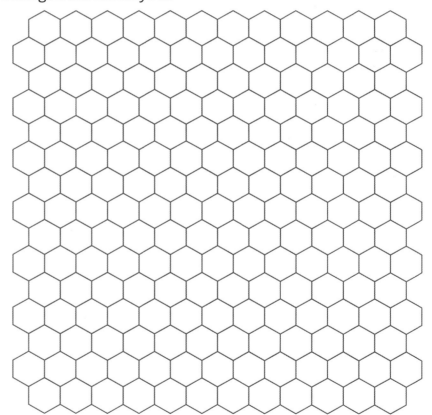

Intarsia Heart Cushion

Intarsia is not as frightening as it may seem! These hearts demonstrate the intarsia method perfectly and are not too big a project to master. They look so pretty in a cushion, which would make a lovely gift for someone who has just moved into a new home. Try out different colour schemes – if you make all the hearts in red it also makes a great Valentine's Day present.

Skills needed:
- **Double crochet**
- **Working in rows**
- **Working intarsia**
- **Joining a new yarn**
- **Double crochet seam**
- **Joining rounds with a slip stitch**

YARN
Debbie Bliss Rialto DK, 100% extra-fine merino DK (light worsted) yarn, approx 105m (115yd) per 50g (1¾oz) ball
- 4 balls of 04 Grey (MC)
- 1 ball each of:
- 09 Apple (green) (A)
- 50 Deep Rose (pink) (B)
- 91 Acid Yellow (yellow) (C)

HOOK AND EQUIPMENT
3.5mm (US size E/4) crochet hook
Yarn sewing needle
40cm (16in) square cushion pad

TENSION
17 sts x 18 rows over a 10cm (4in) square, working double crochet using a 3.5mm (US size E/4) hook.

MEASUREMENTS
Finished cushion cover fits a 40cm (16in) square cushion pad.

ABBREVIATIONS
See page 27.

COLOUR COMBINATIONS
Always use MC as the background colour.
Make three squares with the heart motif in A, three with the heart motif in B and three with the heart motif in C.

Heart squares
(make 9)
Using MC, make 24ch.
Row 1 (RS): 1dc in 2nd ch from hook, 1dc in each ch to end. (23 dc)
Row 2: 1ch (does not count as a st), 1dc in each dc to end. (23 dc)
Rows 3–6: Rep Row 2.
Cont in dc throughout, following chart on page 58 for Rows 7–18 to work the heart motif and using one small ball of MC on each side of the motif. Read the chart from bottom up, working odd-number rows from right to left and even-number rows from left to right.
Using MC only, work 7 rows more in dc.
Fasten off.

Cushion cover back

Using MC, make 70ch.

Row 1: 1dc in 2nd ch from hook, 1dc in each st to end. (69 dc)

Row 2: 1ch (does not count as a st), 1dc in each dc to end. (69 dc)

Rep Row 2 for 4 rows more. Cut MC, but do not fasten off.

Cont in dc, working 67 rows more in a random stripe sequence with colours MC, A, B and C for a total of 73 rows. Alternatively, work the remaining 67 rows of stripes in the following sequence:

6 rows A, 6 rows B, 5 rows C, 4 rows MC, 6 rows A, 5 rows C, 5 rows MC, 6 rows B, 5 rows C, 4 rows MC, 5 rows A, 6 rows B, 4 rows MC.

Fasten off.

Making up and finishing

Using a yarn sewing needle, sew in all yarn ends on the back panel and the heart squares. Then join the heart squares together using MC and a double crochet seam with WS together, so the seams will show on the RS of the cushion. First join together the three squares with A hearts, the three squares with B hearts and the three squares with C hearts, to form the three horizontal rows. Then join the three horizontal rows to make a nine-square front panel – with the A hearts at the top, the B hearts in the middle and the C hearts at the bottom.

With WS together, pin the cushion front and back panels together, leaving the top edge open. Join MC with a ss in top left-hand corner, inserting the hook through front and back pieces. Make 1ch, 3dc in corner st, 23dc evenly along side of each of three squares (missing seam joins), 3dc in corner st, 23dc along bottom of each of three squares (missing seam joins), 3dc in corner st, 23dc evenly along side of each square (missing seam joins). Do not fasten off.

Insert cushion pad, then make 23dc along top of each of three squares (missing seam joins), join with a ss in top of first dc of round. Fasten off.

Heart motif chart

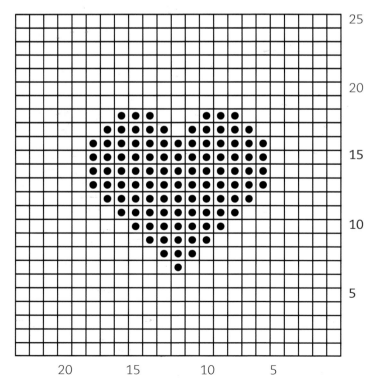

Triangle Blanket

If you are looking for a long-term project that you can just pick up and put down, this blanket is ideal. It's a real special occasion blanket – a true piece of art – so take your time with it. Each motif has the same pattern, but uses a different colour in the centre. I used my favourite silk blend yarn – if you choose something different, don't go thicker than a DK weight.

Skills needed:
- **Treble**
- **Triple treble**
- **Double crochet**
- **Double treble**
- **Working into a ring**
- **Joining rounds with a slip stitch**
- **Working into a chain space**
- **Joining a new yarn**
- **Making a cluster**
- **Raised double crochet round front**
- **Oversewn seam**

YARN
Fyberspates Scrumptious 4-ply Sport, 55% merino wool, 45% silk 4-ply (sportweight) yarn, approx 365m (399yd) per 100g (3½oz) hank
  6 hanks of 304 Water (blue-grey) (MC)
  1 hank each of:
  306 Baby Pink (pale pink) (A)
  315 Magenta (deep pink) (B)
  302 Gold (C)
  311 Flying Saucer (pale green) (D)

HOOK AND EQUIPMENT
3.5mm (US size E/4) crochet hook
Yarn sewing needle

TENSION
Sides of triangle measure 16cm (6¼in) using a 3.5mm (US size E/4) hook.

MEASUREMENTS
Finished blanket measures approx 110 x 144cm (43¼ x 56¾in).

COLOUR COMBINATIONS
Always use MC for Rounds 3, 4 and 5.
Triangle 1: colour 1 = A, colour 2 = B (make 14)
Triangle 2: colour 1 = B, colour 2 = C (make 15)
Triangle 3: colour 1 = B, colour 2 = D (make 10)
Triangle 4: colour 1 = B, colour 2 = A (make 10)
Triangle 5: colour 1 = A, colour 2 = C (make 11)
Triangle 6: colour 1 = A, colour 2 = D (make 12)
Triangle 7: colour 1 = C, colour 2 = B (make 9)
Triangle 8: colour 1 = C, colour 2 = A (make 10)
Triangle 9: colour 1 = C, colour 2 = D (make 11)
Triangle 10: colour 1 = D, colour 2 = B (make 11)
Triangle 11: colour 1 = D, colour 2 = A (make 12)
Triangle 12: colour 1 = D, colour 2 = C (make 11)

ABBREVIATIONS
See page 27.

SPECIAL ABBREVIATIONS
dc/rf (raised double crochet round front): insert hook from front, work 1dc around post of stitch
3trtrCL (3-triple treble cluster): *yrh 3 times, insert hook in sp, yrh, pull yarn through work (5 loops on hook), [yrh, pull yarn through first 2 loops on hook] 3 times; rep from * twice more (4 loops on hook), yrh, pull yarn through all 4 loops on hook

Triangles

(make 136)

Using colour 1, make 4ch and join with a ss in first ch to form a ring.

Round 1 (RS): 5ch (counts as 1tr and 2ch), [1tr into ring, 2ch] 5 times, join with a ss in 3rd of 5-ch at beg of round.

Fasten off colour 1.

Cont in rounds with RS always facing you.

Round 2: Join colour 2 with a ss in top of any tr, *5ch, 3trtrCL in next 2-ch sp, 5ch, 1dc/rf around next tr from previous round; rep from * 5 times more, join with a ss in same sp as joining st. Fasten off colour 2.

Round 3: Join MC with a ss in top of any 3-trtrCL from previous round, 7ch (counts as 1dtr and 3ch), 1dtr in same st (corner), *3ch, 1trtr in next dc/rf, 3ch, 1dc in next 3-trtrCL, 3ch, 1trtr in next dc/rf, 3ch, [1dtr, 3ch, 1dtr] (corner) in next 3-trtrCL; rep from * once more, 3ch, 1trtr in next dc/rf, 3ch, 1dc in next 3-trtrCL, 3ch, 1trtr in next dc/rf, 3ch, join with a ss in 4th of first 7-ch.

Round 4: Ss in next 3-ch sp, 6ch, (counts as 1tr and 3ch), 2tr in same ch sp (corner), *[1tr in next st, 3tr in next ch sp] 4 times**, 1tr in next st, [2tr, 3ch, 2tr] in corner sp*; rep from * to * once more, then work from * to **, 1tr in same place as ss at end of Round 3, 1tr in same sp as ss at beg of round, join with a ss in 3rd of first 6-ch. (21 tr on each side of triangle)

Round 5: Ss in next 3-ch sp, 6ch (counts as 1tr and 3ch), 2tr in same ch sp (corner), *1tr in each tr to next corner sp, [2tr, 3ch, 2tr] in corner sp; rep from * once more, 1tr in each tr to next corner, 1tr in same place as ss at end of Round 4, 1tr in same corner sp as ss at beg of round, join with a ss in third of first 6-ch. (25 tr on each side of triangle)

Fasten off.

Making up and finishing

Lay out all the triangles on a flat surface, making sure that you place the colours randomly and evenly, setting them out in strips as in the layout diagram.

With RS together, join the triangles in strips using an oversewn seam.

Triangle blanket layout

Tip

When you have made all the triangles for the blanket you will be eager to get them joined and the project finished. But these motifs, especially if made using a silk yarn, may be a little out of shape so it's important to sew in all the ends first, then block and steam each triangle on the wrong side before laying out the blanket design.

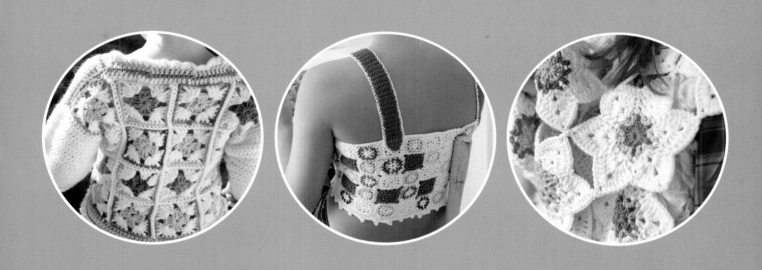

Child's Granny Square Sweater

A warm and cosy jumper suitable for a girl or boy. The squares, based on the traditional granny square, are easy for beginners; the picot and neck shaping are slightly more advanced.

Skills needed:

- Treble
- Double crochet
- Half treble
- Slip stitch
- Working into a ring
- Joining rounds with a slip stitch
- Working into a chain space
- Creating a square
- Joining a new yarn
- Double crochet seam
- Decreasing
- Making a picot

YARN

Rooster Almerino DK, 50% baby alpaca, 50% merino wool DK (light worsted) yarn, approx 113m (124yd) per 50g (1¾oz) ball
  3 balls of 201 Cornish (off white) (MC)
  1 ball each of:
  203 Strawberry Cream (pale pink) (A)
  209 Smoothie (rust) (B)
  205 Glace (pale blue) (C)
  210 Custard (yellow) (D)
  207 Gooseberry (green) (E)
  204 Grape (purple) (F)

HOOK AND EQUIPMENT

4mm (US size F/5) crochet hook
Yarn sewing needle

TENSION

Each square measures approx 6cm (2½in), using a 4mm (US size F/5) hook.
Sleeves measure 20 sts x 14 rows over a 10cm (4in) square, working half treble using a 4mm (US size F/5) hook.

SIZE

To fit age: 12–24 months

MEASUREMENTS

Chest: 57.5cm (22¾in)
Length: 32.5cm (12¾in)
Sleeve seam: 19cm (7½in)

ABBREVIATIONS

See page 27.

COLOUR COMBINATIONS

Use different colour combinations on each square; always use MC for Round 2.

Square

(make 30)
Using first colour, make a loop, make 4ch, join with ss in first ch to form a ring.
Round 1: 3ch, 2tr into ring, 2ch, 3tr into ring, 2ch, *3tr into ring, 2ch; rep from * once more, join with ss in top of first 3-ch.
Fasten off.
Join MC in any ch sp.
Round 2: 3ch, 2tr, 3ch, 3tr in same ch sp (first corner), 2ch, *3tr, 3ch, 3tr in next ch sp, 2ch; rep from * twice more, join with ss in top of first 3-ch.

Fasten off.

Join third colour in fasten-off st, make 1ch.

Round 3: 1dc in each of next 2 sts, 3dc in next ch sp, 1dc in each of next 3 sts, 2dc in next ch sp, *1dc in each of next 3 sts, 3dc in next ch sp, 1dc in each of next 3 sts, 2dc in next ch sp; rep from * twice more, join with ss in first ch.

Fasten off.

Making up and finishing

Sew in ends neatly and securely after making each square.

To make up back, using double crochet seams, join strips of 4 squares across by 4 squares down to make a 16-square panel. For front, join together strips of 4 squares across by 3 squares down to make a 14-square panel. To create a hole for the neck join 1 square on each outside strip (left and right of front).

For the shoulders

Using MC and with RS facing, join yarn in top right-hand corner of front piece and work in tr as follows:

Row 1: 3ch, 1tr in each st across square.

Fasten off.

Row 2: Using A, join yarn at beg (not end) of previous row in top of first 3-ch, 3ch, 1tr in each st across.

Fasten off.

Row 3: Using B, join yarn at beg (not end) of previous row in top of first 3-ch, 3ch, 1tr in each st across.

Fasten off.

Rep on other shoulder, joining yarn and starting at top outside edge. Using a yarn sewing needle and suitable yarn colour, join shoulder seams.

For the neck edging

Using MC and with RS facing, join MC in back of neck at right-hand side of jumper in corner st of shoulder and dc joining seam of square and work in htr as follows:

Round 1: 2ch, 1htr in each st across back (30 sts), 2htr in each colour (row end from shoulders, 6 sts), 1htr in each st down left front edge (11 sts), 1htr in corner seam st, 1htr in next and each st across centre front (27 sts), 1htr in corner seam st, 1htr in next and each st up right front (12 sts), 2htr in each colour (row end from shoulders), 1htr in corner seam (7 sts), join with ss in first 2-ch. (93 sts)

Join in B.

Round 2: 2ch, [1htr in each of next 8 sts, htr2tog] 3 times, 1htr in each of next 2 sts, htr2tog, 1htr in each of next 9 sts, htr2tog, [1htr in each of next 6 sts, htr2tog] 4 times, 1htr in each of next 9 sts, htr2tog, 1htr in each of next 2 sts, htr2tog, 1htr in shoulder seam, join with ss in top of first 2-ch. (83 sts)

Join in C.

Round 3: 2ch, [1htr in each of next 7 sts, htr2tog] 3 times, 1htr in next st, htr2tog, 1htr in each of next 8 sts, [htr2tog] 4 times, 1htr in each of next 6 sts, htr2tog, 1htr in each of next 6 sts, [tr2tog] 4 times, 1htr in each of next 7 sts, htr2tog, 1htr in each of next 2 sts, htr2tog, 1htr in next st, join with ss in top of first 2-ch. (68 sts)

Join in A.

Round 4: 2ch, 1htr in each of next 5 sts, htr2tog, 1htr in each of next 7 sts, htr2tog, 1htr in each of next 7 sts, htr2tog, 1htr in each of next 7 sts, [htr2tog] 3

Front layout

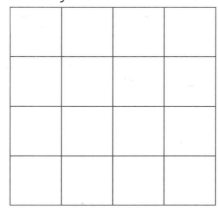

Back layout

times, 1htr in each of next 5 sts, htr2tog, 1htr in each of next 6 sts, [htr2tog] 3 times, 1htr in each of next 7 sts, htr2tog, 1htr in each of next 3 sts, ss in top of first 2-ch. Join in MC.

Round 5 (picot): *3ch, ss in same st, 3ch, ss in next st; rep from * to end.
Fasten off.

For the side edgings
Left side (back):
With RS facing, join MC at side edge of back piece in second square down from shoulder and in centre stitch of square, 1ch, 1dc in each st to bottom edge.
Join in D.
Next row: 1dc in each st to end.
Fasten off.
Left side (front):
With RS facing, join MC in bottom corner st, 1ch, 1dc in each st to centre st of second square from shoulder.
Join in E.
Next row: 1dc in each st to end.
Fasten off.
Right side (back):
With RS facing, join MC at side edge in bottom corner st, 1ch, 1dc in each st to centre st of second square from shoulder.
Join in D.

Next row: 1dc in each st to end.
Fasten off.
Right side (front):
With RS facing, join in E at side edge of front piece, in second square down from shoulder and in centre st of square, 1ch, 1dc in each st to bottom edge.
Join in MC.
Next row: 1dc in each st to end.
Fasten off.

For the bottom edging
With WS facing, join in D in left corner of bottom edge of front, 2ch, 1htr in each row end of side panel, 1htr in each st along bottom edge (of squares), 1htr in each row end of second side panel.
Break yarn. Join in C.
Next row: 2ch, 1htr in each st to end.
Break yarn. Join in B.
Next row: 2ch, 1htr in each st to end.
Break yarn. Join in MC.
Next row (picot): *3ch, 1ss in same st, 1ss in next st; rep from * to end.
Fasten off.
Rep for back. With WS facing, join side panel seams.

For the sleeves
With RS facing, join MC in underarm st at front.

Row 1: 2ch, using htr, make 48 sts evenly around sleeve edge (htr2tog in last sts if necessary to achieve 48 sts), turn.
Row 2: 2ch, 1htr in each st to end, ss in top of first 2-ch, turn.
Row 3: 2ch, 1htr in each st to end, ss in top of first 2-ch, turn.
Row 4: 2ch, 1htr in next st, htr2tog, 1htr in each st to last 3 sts, htr2tog, 1htr in last st, turn. (46 sts)
Row 5: Rep Row 4. (44 sts)
Row 6: Rep Row 4. (42 sts)
Row 7: Rep Row 4. (40 sts)
Row 8: 2ch, 1htr in each st to end, ss in top of first 2-ch, turn.
Row 9: Rep Row 8.
Row 10: Rep Row 4. (38 sts)
Row 11: Rep Row 8.
Row 12: Rep Row 2.
Row 13: Rep Row 4. (36 sts)
Rows 14–15: Rep Row 2.
Row 16: Rep Row 4. (34 sts)
Rows 17–18: Rep Row 2.
Row 19: Rep Row 4. (32 sts)
Rows 20–21: Rep Row 2.
Row 22: Rep Row 4. (30 sts)
Break yarn.
Sleeve cuffs:
Join in D.
Row 1: 1ch, 1dc in first st, *dc2tog, 1dc in each of next 2 sts; rep from * to end, ss in first 1-ch.
Break yarn. Join in C.
Row 2: 1ch, 1dc in each st to end.
Break yarn. Join in B.
Row 3: Rep Row 2.
Break yarn. Join in A.
Row 4: Rep Row 2.
Break yarn. Join in MC.
Row 5: Ss in next st, *3ch, ss in same st, ss in next st; rep from * to end.
Fasten off.
With WS facing, join sleeve seams with a double crochet seam. Sew in ends.

Crop Top

Made with easy little squares that are joined together, this funky and fashionable crop top is a great beginner's project.

Skills needed:
- **Half treble**
- **Double crochet**
- **Slip stitch**
- **Working into a ring**
- **Joining rounds with a slip stitch**
- **Working into a chain space**
- **Creating a square**
- **Joining a new yarn**
- **Working in rows**
- **Double crochet seam**
- **Decreasing**

YARN
Rowan Cotton Glacé, 100% cotton DK (light worsted) yarn, approx 115m (125yd) per 50g (1¾oz) ball
3 balls of 726 Bleached (white) (A)
2 balls of 850 Cobalt (blue) (B)
1 ball each of:
861 Rose (C)
833 Ochre (yellow) (D)
845 Shell (pale pink) (E)
858 Aqua (pale blue) (F)
862 Blackcurrant (G)

HOOK AND EQUIPMENT
2.5mm (US size C/2) crochet hook
Yarn sewing needle

TENSION
Square measures 4cm (1½in) using a 2.5mm (US size C/2) hook.

SIZE
To fit UK sizes:
8–10   12–14

MEASUREMENTS

Bust	cm	80	84
	in	31½	33
Length	cm	38.5	38.5
	in	15¼	15¼

ABBREVIATIONS
See page 27.

Two-colour square
(make 50 for small size, 55 for large size)
Using A, make 4ch, join with ss in first ch to form a ring.
Round 1: 3ch (counts as first htr, 1ch), [1htr, 1ch into ring] 7 times, join with ss in 2nd of 3-ch. (8 htr) Fasten off.
Round 2: Join C, D, E, F or G in any ch sp between htrs, 2ch, 1htr in same ch sp, *[1ch, 1htr, 1ch] in next ch sp, [1htr, 1ch, 1htr] in next ch sp; rep from * to last ch sp, [1ch, 1htr, 1ch] in last ch sp, join with ss in top of 2-ch. Fasten off.
Round 3: Join A in ch sp between any 2-htr group, 2ch, [1dc, 1ch, 2dc] in same ch sp, [1ch, 1dc] in each of next two ch sps, 1ch, *[2dc, 1ch, 2dc, 1ch] in ch sp of next 2-htr group, [1dc, 1ch] in each of next two ch sps; rep from * to end, join with ss in top of 2-ch. Fasten off.

One-colour square
(make 50 for small size, 55 for large size)
Using A or B, make 4ch, join with ss in first ch to form a ring.
Round 1: 3ch (counts as first htr, 1ch), [1htr, 1ch in ring] 7 times, join with ss in 2nd of 3-ch. (8 htr)
Round 2: Ss in next ch sp, 2ch, 1htr in same ch sp, *[1ch, 1htr, 1ch] in next ch sp, [1htr, 1ch, 1htr] in next ch sp; rep from * to last ch sp, [1ch, 1htr, 1ch] in last ch sp, join with ss in top of 2-ch.
Round 3: Ss in next ch sp (between 2-ch and 1htr from Round 2), 2ch, [1dc, 1ch, 2dc] in same ch sp, [1ch, 1dc] in each of next two ch sps, 1ch, *[2dc, 1ch, 2dc, 1ch] in ch sp of next 2-htr group, [1dc, 1ch] in each of next two ch sps; rep from * to end, join with ss in top of 2-ch. Fasten off.

Straps
(make 2)
Using B, make 3ch.
Row 1: 1dc in 2nd ch from hook, 2dc in next ch. (3 sts)
Row 2: 1ch, miss first st, 1dc in each of next 2 sts, 1dc in 1-ch from previous row. (3 sts)
Row 3: 1ch, miss first st, 2dc in next st, 1dc in next st, 2dc in 1-ch from previous row. (5 sts)
Row 4: 1ch, miss first st, 2dc in next st, 1dc in each st to end, 2dc in 1-ch from previous row. (7 sts)

Row 5: 1ch, miss first st, 1dc in each st to end, 1dc in 1-ch from previous row. (7 sts)

Rep Row 5 until work measures 38cm (15in).

Next row: 1ch, miss first st, dc2tog, 1dc in each st to last st, dc2tog over last st and 1-ch from previous row. (5 sts)

Next row: 1ch miss first st, dc2tog, 1dc in next st, dc2tog over last st and 1-ch from previous row. (3 sts)

Next row: 1ch, miss first st, dc2tog, 1dc in 1-ch from previous row. (3 sts)

Next row: Dc3tog.

Fasten off.

Strap edging:

With RS facing, join A in any st on long edge.

Work dc edging evenly all around strap, making 2dc in each end stitch.

Fasten off.

Crochet buttons

(make 2)

Using A, and leaving a tail approx 15cm (6in) long, make 2ch, 5dc in 2nd ch from hook, join with ss in first ch.

Round 1: 1ch, 1dc in next st, 2dc in each st to end, join with ss in first ch.

Round 2: 1ch, 1dc in each st, join with ss in first ch.

Round 3: Dc2tog around.

Fasten off.

Turn inside out. Thread a yarn needle with yarn end, scrunch up starting tail and stuff in centre of button. Weave needle in and out around edge and pull tight to close.

Sew to secure.

Making up and finishing

Arrange squares in 5 rows of 20 (small size); 5 rows of 22 (large size) in the following sequence:

Rows 1, 3 and 5 – alternate one-colour square in A and two-color square.

Rows 2 and 4 – alternate two-colour square and one-colour square in B.

Join squares and rows into a panel, using a double crochet seam, and then join short ends of panel to make a circular top.

For the bottom edging

Round 1: With RS facing, attach A in back seam at bottom edge, 1ch, work dc evenly around edge to end, join with ss in first dc.

Round 2: *3ch, 1dc in first ch, 1dc at base of 3-ch, miss 1 st, dc2tog, 1dc in each of next 3 sts; rep from * to end, join with ss in first dc.

Fasten off.

For the top edging

Round 1: With RS facing, attach A in back seam at top edge, 1ch, work dc evenly around edge, join with ss in first dc.

Fasten off.

Attach the straps to the crop top from front to back. Sew a button to the end of each front strap for decoration. Sew in ends.

Circles Cardigan

This patchwork cardigan is made with circles instead of traditional squares. There are lots like it in vintage markets, but making your own is much more satisfying!

YARN

Rooster Almerino Baby, 50% baby alpaca, 50% merino wool DK (light worsted) yarn, approx 125m (136yd) per 50g (1¾oz) ball

6 balls of 502 Seashell (off white) (A)

1 ball each of:

513 Pebbles (beige) (B)

508 Surf (aquamarine) (C)

504 Seaweed (green) (D)

Debbie Bliss Baby Cashmerino, 55% merino wool, 33% microfibre, 12% cashmere lightweight DK (sportweight) yarn, approx 125m (137yd) per 50g (1¾oz) ball

1 ball each of:

700 Ruby (red) (E)

008 Navy (F)

086 Coral (deep pink) (G)

HOOK AND EQUIPMENT

3.5mm (US size E/4) crochet hook

Yarn sewing needle

TENSION

Each circle is 8cm (3⅛in) in diameter, using a 3.5mm (US size E/4) hook.

SIZE

One size

MEASUREMENTS

Bust: 96cm (37¾in)

Length: 60cm (23½in)

Sleeve seam: 38cm (15in)

ABBREVIATIONS

See page 27.

SPECIAL ABBREVIATION

puff st (puff stitch): [yrh, insert hook in ring, yrh and pull through] twice, yrh and pull through all 5 loops on hook

COLOUR COMBINATIONS

Use either B, C, D, E, F or G for Rounds 1, 2 and 3, changing colour at the end of each round, and A for Round 4.

Circles

(make 128)

Using first colour, make 4ch, join with ss to form a ring.

Round 1: 3ch, 1htr in ring (counts as first puff st), 1ch, [puff st, 1ch] 7 times in ring, join with ss in htr. (8 petals)

Fasten off first colour.

Round 2: Attach 2nd colour in any 1-ch sp, 3ch, 1tr in next ch sp, 2ch, [2tr, 2ch] in each of next 7 ch sps, join with ss in top of 3-ch.

Fasten off 2nd colour.

Round 3: Attach 3rd colour in any 2-ch sp, 3ch, [1tr, 1ch, 2tr, 1ch] in same ch sp, [2tr, 1ch] twice in each of next 7 ch sps, join with ss in top of 3-ch.

Fasten off 3rd colour.

Round 4: Attach A in any 1-ch sp, 3ch, 2tr in same ch sp, 1ch, [3tr, 1ch] in each of next 15 ch sps, join with ss in top of 3-ch.

Fasten off.

Making up and finishing

Sew in ends.

Join circles through corresponding pairs of 3-tr: for each front, join 7 rows each of 3 circles; for the back, join 8 rows each of 6 circles. Join fronts to back at shoulders (top row of back circles sits halfway across shoulders).

Join one row of 5 circles for top of first sleeve, then add two rows of 4 circles and two rows of 3 circles. Join centre circle of 5-circle row of sleeve to circle on shoulder, and 2 circles on either side to corresponding circles on back or front. Join side/sleeve seam. Repeat for sleeve on other side.

To shape neck, turn half of first and 2nd circles at front neck edge under, oversew in place and press to create a neck edge.

Back layout

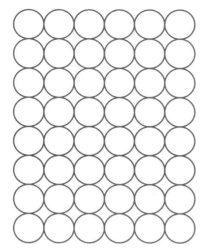

Fronts layout

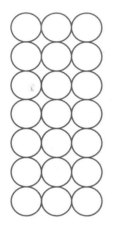

Sleeves layout

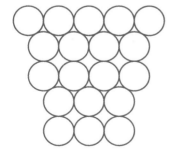

Daisy Scarf

A delicate lace stitch scarf, made using an alpaca yarn. The daisies are entwined into the lace stitch, and then just stitch the squares together to create a lovely, wearable scarf.

Skills needed:
- **Double crochet**
- **Treble**
- **Double treble**
- **Half treble**
- **Working into a ring**
- **Joining rounds with a slip stitch**
- **Decreasing**
- **Working into a chain space**
- **Creating a square**
- **Making a cluster**
- **Joining a new yarn**
- **Oversewn seam**

YARN
Debbie Bliss Baby Cashmerino, 55% merino wool, 33% microfibre, 12% cashmere lightweight DK (sportweight) yarn, approx 125m (137yd) per 50g (1¾oz) ball
  1 ball of 001 Primrose (yellow) (A)
Rooster Almerino Baby, 50% baby alpaca, 50% merino wool DK (light worsted) yarn, approx 125m (136yd) per 50g (1¾oz) ball
  1 ball of 502 Seashell (off white) (B)
  3 balls of 501 Sea Spray (cream) (C)

HOOK AND EQUIPMENT
3mm (US size D/3) crochet hook
Yarn sewing needle

TENSION
Each square measures 11.5 x 11.5cm (4½ x 4½in) using a 3mm (US size D/3) hook.

MEASUREMENTS
Finished scarf measures 153.5 x 15.5cm (60 x 6in).

ABBREVIATIONS
See page 27.

SPECIAL ABBREVIATION
3trCL (3 treble cluster): [yrh, insert hook in st, pull yarn through, yrh, pull through first 2 loops on hook] 3 times in same st, yrh, pull through all 4 loops on hook

Squares
(make 13)
Using A, make 4ch, join with a ss in first ch to form a ring.
Round 1 (RS): 1ch, 8dc into ring, break off A, join in B with a ss in first dc. (8 sts)
Cont in rounds with RS always facing.
Round 2: 3ch, tr2tog in same place as last ss (counts as 3trCL), [3ch, 3trCL in next dc] 7 times, 3ch, join with a ss in top of tr2tog. (8 clusters)
Fasten off B.
Round 3: Join C with a ss in top of any 3-trCL, 3ch, 1tr in same place as ss (counts as tr2tog), *miss 3 ch, [tr2tog, 5ch, tr2tog] in top of next 3-trCL; rep from * 6 more times, tr2tog in same place as first tr of round, 5ch, join with a ss in top of first tr.
Round 4: 7ch, (counts as 1tr and 4ch), [1dc in next 5-ch sp, 4ch, miss 1 3-trCL, 1tr in next 3-trCL, 4ch] 7 times, 1dc in next 5-ch sp, 4ch, join with a ss in 3rd of first 7-ch. (16 ch sps)

Round 5: 1ch, 1dc in same place as last ss, *4ch, miss 4 ch, [1dtr, 4ch, 1dtr] in next dc, 4ch, miss 4 ch, 1dc in next tr, 4ch, miss 4 ch, 1htr in next dc, 4ch, miss 4 ch, 1dc in next tr; rep from * 3 times more omitting dc at end of last rep, join with a ss in first dc.

Round 6: 1ch, 1dc in same place as last ss, 4dc in next ch sp, *[1tr, 3ch, 1tr] in next ch sp (corner), 4dc in next ch sp, 1dc in next dc, 4dc in next ch sp, 1dc in next htr, 4dc in next ch sp, 1dc in next dc, 4dc in next ch sp; rep from * twice more, [1tr, 3ch, 1tr] in next ch sp (corner), 4dc in next ch sp, 1dc in next dc, 4dc in next ch sp, 1dc in next htr, 4dc in next ch sp, join with a ss in first dc.
Fasten off.

Making up and finishing

With RS together oversew squares together along one edge, to make one long line.

For the edging

Round 1 (RS): With RS facing, join C with a ss in top left corner sp, 1ch, 3dc in same sp, then (along first long side of scarf) work *1dc in next tr, 1dc in each dc (19 dc in all) to next corner tr, 1dc in next tr, 1dc in next sp, 1dc in seam, 1dc in next sp (at beg of next square)*; rep from * to * along remaining 12 squares but omitting '1dc in seam, 1dc in next sp' at end of last rep; (along first short side of scarf) work 2dc in same sp as last dc (so there are 3 dc in corner sp), 1dc in next tr, 1dc in each dc (19 dc in all) to next corner tr, 1dc in next tr, 3dc in next sp; (along next long side of scarf) rep from * to * along all 13 squares but omitting '1dc in seam, 1dc in next sp' at end of last

rep; (along next short side of scarf) work 2dc in same sp as last dc (so there are 3 dc in corner sp), 1dc in next tr, 1dc in each dc (19 dc in all) to next corner tr, 1dc in next tr, join with a ss in first dc.
Fasten off.
Cont with RS facing.

Round 2: Join C with a ss to centre dc of any 3-dc corner group, 8ch, (counts as first tr and 5ch), 1tr in 5th ch from hook, miss 2 sts, *1tr in next st, 5ch, 1tr in 5th ch from hook, miss 2 sts; rep from * to next corner, 1tr in centre corner st, 5ch,

1tr in 5th ch from hook, 1tr in same corner st, 5ch, 1tr in 5th ch from hook, miss 2 sts; rep from * to last corner, 1tr in centre corner st (at base of first 3-ch), 5ch, 1tr in 5th ch from hook, join with a ss in 3rd of first 8-ch.
Fasten off.
Sew in ends.

Stars Scarf

Joined up flower motifs make a lovely delicate and unusual scarf. The colours remind me of seaside sweet shops and summer time in Brighton.

Skills needed:
- **Treble**
- **Double crochet**
- **Slip stitch**
- **Working into a ring**
- **Joining rounds with a slip stitch**
- **Working in rounds**
- **Working into a chain space**
- **Joining a new yarn**
- **Oversewn seam**

YARN

Louisa Harding Cassia, 75% superwash merino, 25% nylon DK (light worsted) yarn, approx 133m (145yd) per 50g (1¾oz) ball

4 balls of 102 Ecru (off white) (MC)
1 x ball each of:
108 Lime (green) (A)
103 Chick (yellow) (B)
112 Prince (deep blue) (C)
105 Glacier (pale turquoise) (D)
104 Powder (pale pink) (E)
115 Lipstick (bright pink) (F)
111 Earth (dark brown) (G)
121 Mink (light brown) (H)

COLOUR COMBINATIONS

Always use MC for Rounds 3, 4, 5.
Motif 1: Round 1 = A, Round 2 = B (make 4)
Motif 2: Round 1 = C, Round 2 = D (make 4)
Motif 3: Round 1 = E, Round 2 = F (make 4)
Motif 4: Round 1 = G, Round 2 = H (make 4)
Motif 5: Round 1 = D, Round 2 = C (make 3)
Motif 6: Round 1 = B, Round 2 = A (make 3)
Motif 7: Round 1 = F, Round 2 = E (make 3)
Motif 8: Round 1 = H, Round 2 = G (make 3)

HOOK AND EQUIPMENT

3.5mm (US size E/4) crochet hook
Yarn sewing needle

TENSION

Each motif measures approx 14cm (5½in) tip to tip of petal, using a 3.5mm (US size E/4) hook.

MEASUREMENTS

Finished scarf measures approx 23cm (9in) wide x 184cm (72in) long.

ABBREVIATIONS

See page 27.

Tip

Sew in ends after making each motif, closing the hole in the centre with the first end.

Flower motif

(make 28)

Work on RS throughout.

Using first colour, make 6ch, join with a ss in first ch to form a ring.

Round 1: 3ch (counts as 1tr), 1tr, [2ch, 2tr into ring] 5 times, 2ch, join with a ss in top of first 3-ch. (6 ch sps)

Fasten off first colour.

Round 2: Join 2nd colour in first ch sp, 5ch (counts as 1tr, 2ch), 1tr in same ch sp, 1ch, [1tr, 2ch, 1tr, 1ch in next ch sp] 5 times, join with a ss in third of first 5-ch. (Six 2-ch sps, six 1-ch sps)

Fasten off 2nd colour.

Round 3: Join MC in first 2-ch sp, 3ch (counts as 1tr), [1tr, 2ch, 2tr] in same ch sp, 1dc in next 1-ch sp, *[2tr, 2ch, 2tr] in next 2-ch sp, 1dc in next 1-ch sp; rep from * 4 more times, join with a ss in top of first 3-ch. (6 petals)

Round 4: Ss in first tr, ss in first ch sp, 3ch (counts as 1tr), [2tr, 3ch, 3tr] in same ch sp, *1tr in next tr, miss next tr, 1dc in next dc, miss next tr, 1tr in next tr, [3tr, 3ch, 3tr] in next ch sp; rep from * 4 times more, 1tr in next tr, miss next tr, 1dc in next dc, miss next tr, 1tr in

first ss, join with a ss in top of first 3-ch. (6 petals)

Round 5: 3ch (counts as 1tr), 1tr in each of first 2 tr, *[3tr, 3ch, 3tr] in next ch sp, 1tr in each of next 3 tr, miss next tr, 1dc in next dc, miss next tr, 1tr in each of next 3 tr; rep from * 4 times more, [3tr, 3ch, 3tr] in next ch sp, 1tr in each of next 3 tr, miss next tr, 1dc in next dc, miss next tr, join with a ss in top of first 3-ch. (6 petals)

Fasten off.

Making up and finishing

Block and lightly press each motif on WS.

Lay out motifs in 2 lines, with colours evenly distributed and petal corners touching (see photo). With RS together, pin and oversew the petal corners together. Sew in ends.

Jewel Cowl

Made in a silk yarn in jewel-like hues, this cowl is just perfect for wrapping around the neck. Warm but light, with splashes of colour in the centre of each square.

Skills needed:
- **Double crochet**
- **Treble**
- **Half treble**
- **Working into a ring**
- **Joining rounds with a slip stitch**
- **Working into a chain space**
- **Creating a square**
- **Joining a new yarn**
- **Oversewn seam**

YARN
Fyberspates Scrumptious 4-ply Sport, 55% merino wool, 45% silk 4-ply (sportweight) yarn, approx 365m (399yd) per 100g (3½oz) hank
  2 hanks of 318 Glisten (pale grey) (MC)
  1 hank each of:
  306 Baby Pink (pale pink)
  302 Gold
  311 Flying Saucer (pale green)
  315 Magenta (deep pink)
  304 Water (blue-grey)

HOOK AND EQUIPMENT
3.5mm (US size E/4) crochet hook
Yarn sewing needle

TENSION
Each square measures approx 4.5cm (1¾–2in), using a 3.5mm (US size E/4) hook.

MEASUREMENTS
Finished cowl measures approx 17.5cm (7in) deep x 129.5cm (51in) around (when sewn together), approx 131.5cm (52½in) before seam is joined and after pressing.

ABBREVIATIONS
See page 27.

COLOUR COMBINATIONS
Always using MC in Rounds 2 and 3, make squares in the following colours:
Baby Pink (make 23)
Gold (make 22)
Flying Saucer (make 22)
Magenta (make 23)
Water (make 22)

Squares
(make 112)
Using first colour, make 4ch, join with ss to form a ring.
Round 1: 1ch, 12dc into ring, cut first colour, do not fasten off, join MC with ss in first dc. (12 sts)
Round 2: Cont with MC, 3ch (counts as first tr), 1tr in same st, 2tr in each st to end, join with ss in top of 3-ch. (24 sts)
Round 3: 3ch (counts as 1tr), 2tr in same st (first corner), 1htr in next st, 1dc in each of next 3 sts, 1htr in next st. *3tr in next st (second corner), 1htr in next st, 1dc in each of next 3 sts, 1htr in next st; rep from * twice more (four corners), join with ss in top of first 3-ch. Fasten off.

Making up and finishing
Block and press the squares lightly using a damp cloth.

Set out 112 squares with 28 squares along x 4 squares deep, with the colours evenly spaced and with squares WS facing up. With RS together and MC, join the squares in the sets of 4 squares (112 sets) using an oversewn seam. Join these 112 sets together using MC and in the order set out. Block and press lightly on the WS.
With RS together, join the end seam to create a circle. Turn right side out.

For the edging
With RS facing, join MC in one stitch to the side of the seam. 1ch, 1dc in same st, 1dc in next and each st around top to end. Do not work a dc into the seam. Join with a ss in first dc.
Fasten off.
Rep for the bottom edge.

Tip
When you are using this yarn, always wind hanks into a ball before crocheting.

Triangles Scarf

Crocheting motifs is very satisfying, and triangles are a little more unusual. The triangle motifs on this scarf have a colourful flower centre, which really zings out against the pale grey.

Skills needed:

- **Treble**
- **Double treble**
- **Double crochet**
- **Slip stitch**
- **Working into a ring**
- **Joining rounds with a slip stitch**
- **Working into a chain space**
- **Joining a new yarn**
- **Decreasing**
- **Working round post of stitch below**
- **Oversewn seam**

YARN

Debbie Bliss Cashmerino Aran, 55% merino wool, 33% microfibre, 12% cashmere Aran (worsted) yarn, approx 90m (98yd) per 50g (1¾oz) ball
   4 balls of 027 Stone (pale grey) (MC)
   1 x ball each of:
   047 Aqua (green-blue) (A)
   068 Hot Pink (bright pink) (B)
   603 Baby Pink (pale pink) (C)
   076 Willow (pale green) (D)

HOOK AND EQUIPMENT

5mm (US size H/8) crochet hook
Yarn sewing needle

TENSION

Sides of each triangle measure approx 17.5cm (7in), using a 5mm (US size H/8) hook.

MEASUREMENTS

Finished scarf measures approx 17cm (7in) wide x 160cm (63in) long.

ABBREVIATIONS

See page 27.

SPECIAL ABBREVIATIONS

dc/rf (raised double crochet round front): insert hook from front, work 1dc around post of stitch

COLOUR COMBINATIONS

Always use MC for Rounds 3, 4, 5.
Triangle 1: Round 1 = A, Round 2 = B (make 1)
Triangle 2: Round 1 = A, Round 2 = C (make 1)
Triangle 3: Round 1 = A, Round 2 = D (make 2)
Triangle 4: Round 1 = B, Round 2 = A (make 2)
Triangle 5: Round 1 = B, Round 2 = C (make 1)
Triangle 6: Round 1 = B, Round 2 = D (make 1)
Triangle 7: Round 1 = C, Round 2 = A (make 1)
Triangle 8: Round 1 = C, Round 2 = B (make 2)
Triangle 9: Round 1 = C, Round 2 = D (make 1)
Triangle 10: Round 1 = D, Round 2 = A (make 1)
Triangle 11: Round 1 = D, Round 2 = B (make 1)
Triangle 12: Round 1 = D, Round 2 = C (make 2)

Triangle motif

(make 16)

Using first colour, make 4ch, join with ss in first ch to form a ring.

Round 1: 5ch, [1tr, 2ch] into ring 5 times, ss in third of 5-ch.

Fasten off first colour.

Round 2: Join 2nd colour in any 2-ch sp, *4ch, dtr3tog in next 2-ch sp, 4ch, 1 dc/rf around next tr from previous round; rep from * 5 more times, join with ss in same sp as joining st.

Fasten off 2nd colour.

Round 3: Join MC in top of any dtr-3tog from previous round, 6ch (counts as 1tr and 3ch), 1tr in same st, (corner) *3ch, 1dtr in next dc/rf, 3ch, 1dc in next dtr-3tog, 3ch, 1dtr in next dc/rf, 3ch, **[1tr, 3ch, 1tr] (corner) in next dtr-3tog; rep from * once more, 3ch, 1dtr in next dc/rf, 3ch, 1dc in next dtr-3tog, 3ch, 1dtr in next dc/rf, 3ch, join with ss in 3rd of first 6-ch.

Round 4: Ss in next 3-ch sp, 3ch (counts as 1tr), [1tr, 3ch, 2tr] in same ch sp (corner), *[1tr in next st, 3tr in next ch sp] 4 times, [2tr, 3ch, 2tr] in corner sp; rep from * to end, join with ss in top of first 3-ch. (21 tr on each side of triangle)

Round 5: Ss in first tr, ss in next ch sp, 3ch (counts as 1tr), [1tr, 3ch, 2tr] in same ch sp (corner), *1tr in each st to next corner sp, [2tr, 3ch, 2tr] in corner sp; rep from * to end, join with ss in top of first 3-ch. (25 tr on each side of triangle)

Fasten off.

Making up and finishing

With RS together and using MC, oversew 16 triangles together using the layout diagram below as a guide for positioning, making sure you alternate the colours of the flowers at the centre.

For the edging

With RS facing, join MC in 3-ch sp in tip of one end, 1ch, 3dc in same ch sp, *1dc in each of next 25 sts, (to join) 1dc in each of next 3 sps; rep from * to next tip of scarf, 3dc in ch sp; rep from * to end, join with ss in first dc.

Block and lightly press on WS.

Triangles scarf layout

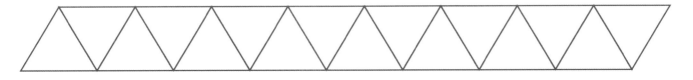

Chunky Squares Scarf

I searched high and low for different square motif designs that would show off this lovely Aran yarn. I made lots of samples, but the one I kept coming back to was the traditional granny square. It's so simple and stylish and this is the perfect project for a beginner.

YARN

Debbie Bliss Cashmerino Aran, 55% merino wool, 33% microfibre, 12% cashmere Aran (worsted) yarn, approx 90m (98yd) per 50g (1¾oz) ball

3 balls of 09 Grey (MC)
2 balls of 101 Ecru (A)
1 ball each of:
075 Citrus (yellow)
603 Baby Pink (pale pink)
072 Peach
048 Burnt Orange
047 Aqua (mid blue-green)
081 Mint (pale green)
061 Jade (bright green)
062 Kingfisher (bright blue)
056 Mallard (dark teal)
073 Coral (mid-orange)

HOOK AND EQUIPMENT

4.5mm (US size 7) crochet hook
Yarn sewing needle

TENSION

Each square measures approx 12.5cm (5in), using a 4.5mm (US size 7) hook.

MEASUREMENTS

Finished scarf measures approx 26.5cm (10½in) wide x 217cm (85½in) long.

ABBREVIATIONS

See page 27.

COLOUR COMBINATIONS

Use A for Round 4
Use MC for Round 5
Use a mixture of other colours for Rounds 1 to 3.

Square

(make 30)
Work on RS throughout.
Using first colour, make 4ch, join with ss in first ch to form a ring.
Round 1 (RS): 3ch (counts as first tr), 2tr, 2ch into ring, [3tr, 2ch into ring] 3 times, join with ss in third of first 3-ch. (Four 3-tr groups)
Fasten off first colour.
Round 2: Join 2nd colour with ss in any 2-ch, 3ch (counts as first tr), [2tr, 2ch, 3tr] in same 2-ch sp (corner), *1ch, [3tr, 2ch, 3tr] in next ch sp; rep from * twice more, 1ch, join with ss in third of first 3-ch. (4 corners)

Fasten off 2nd colour.
Round 3: Join 3rd colour with ss in any corner 2-ch sp, 3ch (counts as first tr), [2tr, 2ch, 3tr] in same 2-ch sp, *1ch, 3tr in next 1-ch sp, 1ch, [3tr, 2ch, 3tr] in next 2-ch sp; rep from * twice more, 1ch, 3tr in next 1-ch sp, 1ch, join with ss in third of first 3-ch.
Fasten off 3rd colour.
Round 4: Join A with ss in any corner 2-ch sp, 3ch (counts as first tr), [2tr, 2ch, 3tr] in same 2-ch sp, *[1ch, 3tr in next 1-ch sp] twice, 1ch, [3tr, 2ch, 3tr] in next 2-ch sp; rep from * twice more, [1ch, 3tr in next 1-ch sp] twice, 1ch, join with ss in third of first 3-ch.
Fasten off A.
Round 5: Join MC with ss in any corner 2-ch sp, 3ch (counts as first tr), [2tr, 2ch, 3tr] in same 2-ch sp, *[1ch, 3tr in next 1-ch sp] 3 times, 1ch, [3tr, 2ch, 3tr] in next 2-ch sp; rep from * twice more, [1ch, 3tr in next 1-ch sp] 3 times, 1ch, join with ss in third of first 3-ch.
Fasten off.

Making up and finishing

Sew in ends.

Arrange the squares in 15 pairs. With WS together, using MC, join seams up centre length using a double crochet seam, and then across each width. After seams are joined, join yarn on RS of work at one end, 1ch, make 1dc in each st along end of scarf. Fasten off.

Rep at other end of scarf.

Tip

If you don't feel like sewing in ends after each square, then at least sew in after two or three.

CHAPTER 3

TO *Carry* AND *Cover*

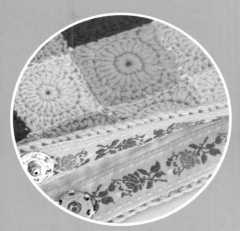

Patchwork Bag

This patchwork bag is made in bright squares and stripes set against white, with felted flowers to decorate. A fabric lining will make the bag stronger, but is not essential.

● ●

YARN

Rooster Almerino Aran, 50% baby alpaca, 50% merino wool Aran (worsted) yarn, approx 94m (103yd) per 50g (1¾oz) ball
3 balls of 301 Cornish (off white) (A)
1 ball each of:
306 Gooseberry (green) (B)
307 Brighton Rock (pink) (C)
314 Damson (purple) (D)
310 Rooster (red) (E)
305 Custard (yellow) (F)
311 Deep Sea (blue) (G)
Cascade 220, 100% Peruvian highland wool Aran (worsted) yarn, approx 200m (220yd) per 100g (3½oz) hank
1 hank of 9404 Ruby (deep pink) (H)

HOOK AND EQUIPMENT

4.5mm (US size 7) crochet hook
Yarn sewing needle
Fabric to line bag
Sewing needle and thread

TENSION

Each square measures 11cm (4¼in), using a 4.5mm (US size 7) hook.

MEASUREMENTS

Finished bag measures approx 41.5 x 35cm (16½ x 13¾in).

ABBREVIATIONS

See page 27.

SPECIAL ABBREVIATION

dtrCL (double treble cluster): yrh twice, insert yarn in sp, pull yarn through work, yrh, pull yarn through 2 loops (3 loops on hook), *yrh twice, insert hook in same sp, pull yarn through work, yrh, pull yarn through 2 loops (5 loops on hook); rep from * twice (9 loops on hook), yrh, pull yarn through all 9 loops on hook, 1ch

Front and back panels

(make 12 squares, 2 in each colour for Round 2)
Using A, make 6ch, join with ss in first ch to form a ring.
Round 1: 4ch (counts as first dtr), 11dtr in ring, join with ss in top of first 4-ch. (12 dtr)
Fasten off A. Join 2nd colour in first sp.
Round 2: 4ch, yrh twice, insert hook in first sp, pull yarn through work, yrh, pull yarn through 2 loops (3 loops on hook), *yrh twice, insert hook in same sp, pull yarn through work, yrh, pull yarn through 2 loops (5 loops on hook); rep from * once more (7 loops on

hook), yrh, pull through all 7 loops, 1ch (counts as first dtrCL), 1dtrCL in the next and each sp to end of round, join with a ss in top of first dtrCL. (12 dtrCL)
Fasten off 2nd colour. Join A in any ch sp.
Round 3: 4ch (counts as first dtr), [2dtr, 3ch, 3dtr] in same sp, *[3dtr in next sp] twice, [3dtr, 3ch, 3dtr] in next sp; rep from * twice more, [3dtr in next sp] twice, join with ss in top of first 4-ch.
Round 4: 1ch, *1dc in each st to corner, 3dc in corner ch sp, rep from * 3 times more, 1dc in each st, join with ss in first dc.
Fasten off.
Take one of each pair of squares with WS together and join in 2 horizontal rows of 3, using double crochet seam on RS. Fasten off after joining each pair of squares and leave the centre of 3-dc unjoined where four squares meet. Repeat with remaining squares, so front and back panel of bag are the same.

Panel base

(make 2)
Mark top and bottom of each panel. Working on bottom edge of first panel with RS facing, join A in centre st of 3-dc at first corner, *1dc in each of next 14 dc, 1dc in

seam; rep from * once more, 1dc in each of next 15 dc along last square. (46 sts)
Fasten off A.
Join B in first st. Work all rows with RS facing.
Row 1: 3ch (counts as first tr), 2tr in same st, 1ch, * miss 2 sts, 3tr in next st; rep from * to end.
Fasten off B. Join C at beg of last row between first 3-ch and first st.
Row 2: 3ch, 3tr in next and each sp, ending 3tr in last sp, 3ch, ss in top of last 3-tr from previous row.
Fasten off C. Join D in first 3-ch sp at beg of previous row.
Row 3: 3ch, 2tr in same sp, 3tr in next and each sp, ending 3tr in last ch sp.
Fasten off D.
Rep Row 2 using E and Row 3 using F, then rep Row 2 again using G.
Fasten off.

Sides and bottom
Using B, make 164ch.
Row 1: 1dc in 2nd ch from hook, 1dc in each ch to end. (163 sts)
Row 2: 1ch, 1dc in each st to end. Fasten off B, join A.
Row 3: 1ch, 1dc in each st to end. Fasten off A, join C.
Row 4: 1ch, 1dc in each st to end.
Row 5: 1ch, 1dc in each st to end. Fasten off C, join A.
Rows 6–26: Rep Rows 3–5, always working Row 3 in A and working Rows 4 and 5 in the following order: D, F, E, G, B, C and D.
Fasten off.

Handles
(make 2)
Using B, make 107ch.
Row 1: 1dc in 2nd ch from hook, 1dc in each ch to end. (106 sts)
Row 2: 1ch, 1dc in each st to end. Fasten off B, join C.
Rep Row 2, changing colour every 2 rows in same order as bag sides and bottom (not using A), until a total of 12 rows have been worked.
Fasten off.

Making up and finishing
Before joining, use front and back panels, together with the bag sides and bottom, as a guide to cut the fabric for the lining, allowing an extra 5cm (2in) for the top edging, plus 1cm (½in) extra all around for seams. Allowing 1cm (½in) extra all around for seams, cut the fabric lining for the handles.

Mark the centre on each side of the sides and bottom piece. Mark the centre of each panel base. With RS facing, match marks and pin the sides and bottom piece to the base and sides of each panel. With RS together, join with a double crochet seam on the WS.

For the top edging
Round 1: Using A and with RS facing, join yarn in top right-hand corner of end square. 1dc in each st across first 3 squares, 1dc in each st across first side panel, 1dc in each st across second 3 squares, 1dc in each st across side panel, join with a ss in first dc.
Cont making 1dc in each st around until edging measures 5cm (2in) deep.
Fasten off.

Lining
With RS together, sew the bag lining pieces together, leaving the top open. Sew the handle lining to the WS of each handle, turning the raw edges under as you work. Sew the handles to the top of the top edging of the bag to align with the corner edge of a square. Push the fabric lining into the bag, with WS together, and oversew the lining to the bag around the top opening, turning the raw edges of the lining under as you work.

Flowers
(make 6)
Using H, make 5ch, join with ss to make a ring.
Round 1: *1dc, 1tr, 1dc into ring; rep from * 3 more times. (4 petals)
Round 2: *2ch, from WS ss in base of 2nd dc of next petal (pick up 2 loops); rep from * 3 more times, ss in first 2-ch. (4 loops)
Round 3: *4tr in next 2-ch sp at back, ss in same ch sp; rep from * 3 more times.
Fasten off.
Place flowers in washing machine on 60°C wash. Allow to dry naturally. Sew flowers around top edge of bag.

Sunglasses Case

I'm constantly leaving my sunglasses around and getting them scratched. This case will protect your shades and is a really fun project to make over the summer.

Skills needed:
- **Treble**
- **Double crochet**
- **Working into a ring**
- **Joining rounds with a slip stitch**
- **Joining a new yarn**
- **Working into a chain space**
- **Making a cluster**
- **Creating a square**
- **Oversewn seam**
- **Adding a lining**

YARN
Louisa Harding Cassia, 75% superwash merino, 25% nylon DK (light worsted) yarn, approx 133m (145yd) per 50g (1¾oz) ball
1 ball each of:
124 Coral (deep pink) (A)
105 Glacier (pale turquoise) (B)
104 Powder (pale pink) (C)
107 Lilac (D)
112 Prince (deep blue) (E)

HOOK AND EQUIPMENT
3mm (US size D/3) crochet hook
Yarn sewing needle
Approx 56 x 13cm (22 x 5¼in) of cotton lining fabric
Sewing needle and thread

TENSION
Each square measures 7cm (2¾in), using a 3mm (US size D/3) hook.

MEASUREMENTS
Finished case measures approx 25 x 10cm (10 x 4in).

ABBREVIATIONS
See page 27.

SPECIAL ABBREVIATION
2trCL (2 treble cluster): yrh, insert hook in st or sp, yrh, pull yarn through work (3 loops on hook), yrh, pull yarn through 2 loops on hook (2 loops on hook), yrh, insert hook in same st or sp, yrh, pull yarn through work (4 loops on hook), yrh, pull yarn through 2 loops on hook (3 loops on hook), yrh, pull yarn through all 3 loops on hook

COLOUR COMBINATIONS
Use either A, B, C or D for Rounds 1, 2 and 3 and always use E for Round 4.

Squares
(make 9)
Using A, make 6ch, join with a ss in first ch to form a ring.
Round 1 (RS): 4ch, [1tr, 1ch into ring] 11 times, join with a ss in third of first 4-ch.
Cut yarn, do not fasten off.
Round 2: Join B in next 1-ch sp, 3ch, 1tr in same ch sp, [3ch, 2trCL in next ch sp] 11 times, 3ch, join with a ss in top of first 3-ch. (Twelve 2trCL)
Cut yarn, do not fasten off.
Round 3: Join C in top of next 2tr-CL, 1ch, 1dc in same st, 1ch, miss first 3-ch sp and 2-trCL, *[3tr, 3ch, 3tr in next ch sp] (corner), 1ch, miss next 2-trCL and next 3-ch sp, 1dc in top of next 2-trCL, 1ch, miss next 3-ch sp and next 2-trCL; rep from * 3 times more, ending last rep with a ss in top of first dc.
Cut yarn, do not fasten off.
Round 4: Join D in same dc, 1ch, 1dc in same st, 1dc in first ch sp, *1dc in each of next 3 sts, 3dc in corner ch sp, 1dc in each of next 3 sts, 1dc in next ch sp, 1dc in next dc, 1dc in next ch sp; rep from * 3 times more, 1dc in each of next 3 sts, 3dc in corner ch sp, 1dc in

each of next 3 sts, 1dc in next ch sp, join with a ss in first dc. Fasten off.

Making up and finishing

Block and press squares lightly.

Place the squares on a flat surface and arrange following the layout diagram (right). With RS together, oversew the squares to join into the shaped piece.

Fold the strip of lining fabric in half and make up the lining (see page 26).

Fold the crocheted piece into the glasses cosy shape along the dotted lines, matching the letters. With RS together, pin and then oversew the seams. Turn RS out. Block and press again.

Push the lining inside the cosy, with WS together, and slip stitch the lining to the crochet around the top opening.

Sunglasses case layout

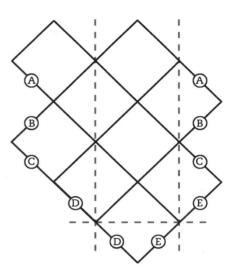

Multicoloured Laptop Cover

A great piece of patchwork to show off and protect your laptop – make as many squares as you need to cover the size. Here I've used the colours in Debbie Bliss Baby Cashmerino, because the shades are very on-trend and it feels very soft to carry around.

Skills needed:
- **Double crochet**
- **Treble**
- **Half treble**
- **Working into a ring**
- **Joining rounds with a slip stitch**
- **Working into a chain space**
- **Creating a square**
- **Oversewn seam**
- **Adding a lining**

YARN
Debbie Bliss Baby Cashmerino, 55% merino wool, 33% microfibre, 12% cashmere lightweight DK (sportweight) yarn, approx 125m (137yd) per 50g (1¾oz) ball

Squares

1 ball each of:
700 Ruby (dark red)
202 Light Blue
094 Rose Pink (pale pink)
003 Mint (pale green)
316 Mustard (bronze)
091 Acid Yellow
101 Ecru (off white)
065 Clotted Cream (cream)
204 Baby Blue (mid-blue)
057 Mist (grey)

Top edging

1 ball of 202 Light Blue

HOOK AND EQUIPMENT
2.5mm (US size C/2) crochet hook
Yarn sewing needle
2 pieces of lining fabric, each approx 45 x 35cm (18 x 14in)
1m (1yd) of 2.5cm (1in) wide ribbon
Snap fastener, 2cm (¾in) diameter

TENSION
Each square measures approx 4.5cm (1¾in), using a 2.5mm (US size C/2) hook.

MEASUREMENTS
Approx 40cm (15¾in) wide x 30cm (12in) long, to fit a Macbook Pro measuring 36.5cm (14½in) wide x 25cm (10in) long x 1cm (½in) deep.

ABBREVIATIONS
See page 27.

COLOUR COMBINATIONS
Make total of 126 squares in the following colours:
Red x 14
Pale blue x 14
Pale pink x 14
Pale green x 14
Bronze x 14
Yellow x 14
Off white x 13
Cream x 12
Mid-blue x 10
Grey x 7

Squares

Make 4ch, join with a ss to form a ring.

Round 1 (RS): 1ch, 12dc into ring, join with a ss in first dc. (12 sts)

Round 2: 3ch (counts as first tr), 1tr in same st, 2tr in each st to end, join with a ss in first tr. (24 sts)

Round 3: 3ch (counts as 1tr), 2tr in same st (first corner), 1htr in next st, 1dc in each of next 3 sts, 1htr in next st. *3tr in next st (second corner), 1htr in next st, 1dc in each of next 3 sts, 1htr in next st; rep from * twice more (four corners), join with a ss in top of first 3-ch. Fasten off.

Making up and finishing

Block and press all the squares.

Set out the front with 9 squares across (width) x 7 down (length), with the colours evenly spaced and with the squares RS facing up. Join in strips with RS together, first vertically then horizontally, using a neutral colour yarn. Press. Rep for the back. With RS together, join the sides and bottom seams of the front and back, leaving the top open. Turn RS out.

For the top edging

With RS facing, join A in a st to side of one seam. 1ch, 1dc in same st, 1dc in next and in each st around top to end, join with a ss in first dc.
Fasten off.

For the lining

Make and insert the lining following the instructions on page 26. Cut the length of ribbon in half and attach one end of each piece at the top edge of the lining on either side, before slip stitching the crochet and lining together. Sew the snap fastener to the ribbon at the mid-point.

Patchwork Sewing Machine Cover

This is a much nicer cover for a sewing machine than the plastic ones that usually come with it. Customise your own sewing machine by making this cosy with crochet squares joined together with a double crochet seam. This doesn't need lining, but a lining will prevent the cotton reel holder from poking through the holes of the crochet stitches.

Skills needed:

- **Treble**
- **Double crochet**
- **Slip stitch**
- **Half treble**
- **Working into a ring**
- **Joining rounds with a slip stitch**
- **Working into a chain space**
- **Creating a square**
- **Double crochet seam**
- **Adding a lining**

YARN

Debbie Bliss Baby Cashmerino, 55% merino wool, 33% microfibre, 12% cashmere lightweight DK (sportweight) yarn, approx 125m (137yd) per 50g (1¾oz) ball
2 balls of 101 Ecru (off white) (A)
1 ball each of:
305 Blush (peach) (B)
018 Citrus (green) (C)
091 Acid Yellow (yellow) (D)
059 Mallard (teal blue) (E)
202 Light Blue (pale blue) (F)

HOOK AND EQUIPMENT

4mm (US size G/6) crochet hook
Yarn sewing needle
½m (½yd) of cotton fabric
Sewing needle and thread

TENSION

Each square measures approx 10cm (4in), using a 4mm (US size G/6) hook.

MEASUREMENTS

To fit a standard-sized sewing machine, 40 x 30 x 10cm (16 x 12 x 4in).

ABBREVIATIONS

See page 27.

COLOUR COMBINATIONS

Make a total of 34 squares in the following colours:
Off white x 5
Peach x 6
Green x 5
Yellow x 6
Teal blue x 5
Pale blue x 7

Squares

Make 6ch, join with a ss to form a ring.

Round 1 (RS): 3ch (counts as 1tr), 15tr into ring, join with a ss in top of first 3-ch. (16 sts)

Round 2: 4ch (counts as 1tr, 1ch), [1tr, 1ch] in next st 15 times, join with a ss in third of first 4-ch. (16 tr)

Round 3: 3ch, *1tr in next ch sp, 1tr in next st; rep from * to end, ending 1tr in last ch sp, join with a ss in top of first 3-ch. (32 tr)

Round 4: 3ch (counts as 1tr), [4tr, 3ch, 5tr] in same place as ss (corner), miss 2 sts, 1dc in next st, 5tr in next st, 1dc in next st, miss 2 sts, *[5tr, 3ch, 5tr] in next st (corner), miss 2 sts, 1dc in next st, 5tr in next st, 1dc in next st, miss 2 sts; rep from * to end, join with a ss in top of first 3-ch.

Round 5: 4ch, miss first 5 tr, 1dc in corner ch sp, 1ch, 1dc in same ch sp, 4ch, miss next 5 tr, 1dc in next dc, 4ch, miss 5 tr, 1dc in next dc,

*4ch, miss next 5 tr, 1dc in corner ch sp, 1ch, 1dc in same ch sp, 4ch, miss next 5 tr, 1dc in next dc, 4ch, miss 5 tr, 1dc in next dc; rep from * ending last rep with ss in base of first 4-ch.

Round 6: Ss in first ch sp, 2ch (counts as first htr), 4htr in same ch sp, *[3htr, 1ch, 3htr] in next 1-ch sp (corner), [5htr in next ch sp] 3 times; rep from * ending last rep with 5htr in each of last 2-ch sps, join with a ss in top of first 2-ch. Fasten off.

Making up and finishing

Block and press squares lightly. Lay out the squares with 4 squares across by 3 squares down, placing the colours randomly. With WS together make double crochet seams, joining the squares together into a panel for the front. Repeat to make another panel for the back.

Join 2 vertical rows of 3 squares for the side panels.

Join 1 horizontal row of 4 squares for the top panel.

With WS together, join one side of the top panel to the front and the other side to the back.

With WS together, add the first side panel, starting at the bottom edge of the front, along the top edge and down the back edge. Repeat on the other side.

Make up a lining in cotton fabric (see page 26). Insert the lining into the cover with WS together. Turn over the hem of the lining at the bottom edge and pin in place around the open edge of the crochet piece. Oversew the lining to the crochet.

Suppliers

UK STOCKISTS

DERAMORES
(yarn, crochet hooks, accessories)
0845 519 4573 or 01795 668144
www.deramores.com
customer.service@deramores.com

DESIGNER YARNS
(distributor for Debbie Bliss yarns)
www.designeryarns.uk.com

FYBERSPATES LTD
(yarn, crochet hooks)
01244 346653
www.fyberspates.co.uk
fyberspates@btinternet.com

HOBBYCRAFT
(yarn, crochet hooks)
Stores nationwide
0330 026 1400
www.hobbycraft.co.uk

LAUGHING HENS
(yarn, accessories)
The Croft Stables
Station Lane
Great Barrow
Cheshire CH3 7JN
01829 740903
www.laughinghens.com
sales@laughinghens.com

JOHN LEWIS
(yarn, crochet hooks, accessories)
Stores nationwide
03456 049049
www.johnlewis.com

Tuition

NICKI TRENCH
Crochet Club, workshops,
accessories
www.nickitrench.com
nicki@nickitrench.com

Accessories

ADDI NEEDLES
(crochet hooks)
01529 240510
www.addineedles.co.uk
addineedles@yahoo.co.uk

KNIT PRO
(crochet hooks)
www.knitpro.eu

US STOCKISTS

KNITTING FEVER
(Debbie Bliss yarns)
Stores nationwide
www.knittingfever.com

THE KNITTING GARDEN
(Debbie Bliss yarns)
www.theknittinggarden.org

WEBS
(yarn, crochet hooks, accessories,
tuition)
75 Service Center Rd
Northampton, MA 01060
1-800-367-9327
www.yarn.com
customerservice@yarn.com

Accessories

A.C. MOORE
(crochet hooks, accessories)
Online and east coast stores
1-888-226-6673
www.acmoore.com

HOBBY LOBBY
(crochet hooks, accessories)
Online and stores nationwide
1-800-888-0321
www.hobbylobby.com

**JO-ANN FABRIC AND CRAFT
STORE**
(crochet hooks, accessories)
Stores nationwide
1-888-739-4120
www.joann.com

MICHAELS
(crochet hooks, beads)
Stores nationwide
1-800-642-4235
www.michaels.com

Index

abbreviations 27

babies and children
Baby Cloths 42–43
Buggy Blanket 47–49
Child's Granny Square Sweater 66–69
Sweetheart Blanket 40–41
backstitch 25
bags, cases and covers
lining with fabric 26–27
Multicoloured Laptop Cover 90–91
Patchwork Bag 86–87
Patchwork Sewing Machine Cover
92–93
Sunglasses Case 88–89
blankets and throws
Buggy Blanket 47–49
Camellia Blanket 34–36
Hexagon Blanket 54–56
Hexagon Flower Throw 44–46
Sweetheart Blanket 40–41
Triangle Blanket 60–63
blocking 25
Buggy Blanket 47–49
Bunting 30–31

Camellia Blanket 34–36
chain (ch) 12
chain ring 12
working into a ring 13
chain space (ch sp) 12
Child's Granny Square Sweater 66–69
Chunky Squares Scarf 82–83
Circles Cardigan 72–73
cloths
Baby Cloths 42–43
Oven Cloths 50–51
Wash Cloth 32–33
clusters 22
three-treble cluster (3trCL) 22
two-treble cluster (2trCL) 22
Crop Top 70–71
Crown-edged Cushion Cover 37–39
cushions
Crown-edged Cushion Cover 37–39
Intarsia Heart Cushion 57–59

Daisy Scarf 74–75
decreasing 20

double crochet (dc) 17, 18
double crochet seam 25
double treble (dtr) 18

equipment 8–9

fabric
backing with 26
lining with 26–27
fastening off 24
front post crochet 19

half treble crochet (htr) 17, 18
Hexagon Blanket 54–56
Hexagon Flower Throw 44–46
holding
hook 10
hook, yarn and crochet 11
yarn 10
hooks 8
holding 10

increasing 20
intarsia 23–24
Intarsia Heart Cushion 57–59

Jewel Cowl 78–79
joining new yarn
after fastening off 16
at end of row or round 16
jumpers and cardigans
Child's Granny Square Sweater 66–69
Circles Cardigan 72–73
Crop Top 70–71

left-handed crocheters 11
loop stitch 20

Multicoloured Laptop Cover 90–91

Oven Cloths 50–51

Patchwork Bag 86–87
Patchwork Sewing Machine Cover 92–93
picot 21
pins 9
puff stitch 21

rounds
joining with slip stitch 15
making rounds 14
working in rounds 14
rows, making 14

scarves and cowls
Chunky Squares Scarf 82–83
Daisy Scarf 74–75
Jewel Cowl 78–79
Stars Scarf 76–77
Triangles Scarf 80–81
scissors 9
seams
double crochet seam 25
oversewn seam 26
slip knot 11
slip stitch (ss) 13, 15
squares
creating 15
tension (gauge) squares 17
Stars Scarf 76–77
stitch conversion chart 27
stitch markers 9, 14
Sunglasses Case 88–89
suppliers 94
Sweetheart Blanket 40–41

tape measure 9
techniques 10–27
tension (gauge) squares 17
treble (tr) 18
Triangle Blanket 60–63
Triangles Scarf 80–81
triple treble (trtr) 19

Vintage-style Vase Coaster 52–53

Wash Cloth 32–33
working into
a ring 13
top of stitch 13

yarn 8
enclosing a yarn tail 16
holding 10
joining 16
sewing in yarn ends 24
yarn round hook (yrh) 11
yarn sewing needles 9

Acknowledgements

A big thank you to Cindy Richards, the publisher of CICO Books, for commissioning me to write the books that all these patterns are taken from; to Penny Craig for doing a fabulous job of project managing; and to Sally Powell and the rest of the team at CICO books for putting together such a lovely book. Thank you to the models, stylist, and photographer for doing such a great job too. And thanks to Alison Fenton for her beautiful design and Stephen Dew for the very clear techniques artworks.

Thank you to Jane Czaja, who did a superb job on the pattern checking. Thanks also to Marie Clayton, who as always, has made an exceptional job of the editing.

I always have a fabulous team of reliable and expert crocheters who help get these patterns produced and made in time for the photography deadlines. They are: Michelle Bull, Duriye Aydin, Jane Czaja, Sian Warr, and Beryl Oakes, my mother, who is well into her eighties but still sewing in ends and crocheting well into the night to help me produce so many beautiful projects.

I always like to work with only the best yarns and I have some really great suppliers. Special thanks to Graeme Knowles-Miller and Rhiannon Evans from Designer Yarns who are exceptionally quick at getting the yarns out and are very really helpful. Thanks also to Jeni Hewlett from Fyberspates for her gorgeous silk yarns.